Racing the Beam

Platform Studies
Ian Bogost and Nick Montfort, editors

Racing the Beam: The Atari Video Computer System, Nick Montfort and Ian Bogost, 2009

Racing the Beam

The Atari Video Computer System

Nick Montfort and Ian Bogost

The MIT Press   Cambridge, Massachusetts   London, England

For information about special quantity discounts, please email special_sales@mitpress.mit.edu

This book was set in Filosofia and Helvetica Neue by SNP Best-set Typesetter Ltd., Hong Kong.

Printed and bound in the United States of America.

Library of Congress Cataloging-in-Publication Data

Montfort, Nick.
  Racing the beam : the Atari video computer system / Nick Montfort and Ian Bogost.
    p. cm — (Platform studies)
  Includes bibliographical references and index.
  ISBN 978-0-262-01257-7 (hardcover : alk. paper)   1. Video games—Equipment and supplies.
2. Atari 2600 (Video game console)   3. Computer games—Programming.   4. Video games—
United States—History.   I. Bogost, Ian.   II. Title.
  TK6681.M65 2009
  794.8—dc22

                                                                                    2008029410

10 9 8 7 6 5 4 3 2 1

Contents

Series Foreword

How can someone create a breakthrough game for a mobile phone or a compelling work of art for an immersive 3D environment without understanding that the mobile phone and the 3D environment are different sorts of computing platforms? The best artists, writers, programmers, and designers are well aware of how certain platforms facilitate certain types of computational expression and innovation. Likewise, computer science and engineering has long considered how underlying computing systems can be analyzed and improved. As important as scientific and engineering approaches are, and as significant as work by creative artists has been, there is also much to be learned from the sustained, intensive, humanistic study of digital media. We believe it is time for those of us in the humanities to seriously consider the lowest level of computing systems and to understand how these systems relate to culture and creativity.

The Platform Studies book series has been established to promote the investigation of underlying computing systems and how they enable, constrain, shape, and support the creative work that is done on them. The series investigates the foundations of digital media: the computing systems, both hardware and software, that developers and users depend upon for artistic, literary, gaming, and other creative development. Books in the series certainly vary in their approaches, but they all also share certain features:

- a focus on a single platform or a closely related family of platforms
- technical rigor and in-depth investigation of how computing technologies work

- an awareness of and discussion of how computing platforms exist in a context of culture and society, being developed based on cultural concepts and then contributing to culture in a variety of ways—for instance, by affecting how people perceive computing

Acknowledgments

We are very grateful for all of the work that was done by the original developers of the Atari VCS and by the programmers of cartridges for that system. We also thank those who replied to our questions about game development on the system and emulation of the system: Bill Bracy, Rex Bradford, David Crane, Jeff Vavasour, and Howard Scott Warshaw.

Thanks to those who helped us to formulate these ideas about the Atari VCS and about platform studies, including Kyle Buza, Chris Crawford, Mark Guzdial, D. Fox Harrell, Steven E. Jones, Matthew G. Kirschenbaum, Jane McGonigal, Jill Walker Rettberg, and Jim Whitehead.

We greatly appreciate the work that Roger Bellin and Dexter Palmer did in organizing the Form, Culture, and Video Game Criticism conference at Princeton University on 6 March 2004. This conference prompted the first scholarship leading to this book. Thanks also to students in Ian Bogost's Videogame Design and Analysis class on the Atari VCS (Georgia Tech, Spring 2007): Michael Biggs, Sarah Clark, Rob Fitzpatrick, Mark Nelson, Nirmal Patel, Wes St. John, and Josh Teitelbaum. Thanks as well to Peter Stallybrass and the participants in his History of Material Texts Workshop at the University of Pennsylvania.

We greatly appreciate the work of modern-day Atari VCS programmers and analysts, which has made our study of the system easier and has allowed us to continue to enjoy the console in new ways. Particular thanks go to the moderators and contributors to the AtariAge forums.

A shout-out goes to the bloggers and readers of *Grand Text Auto*, where much useful discussion of the Atari VCS has transpired.

We also want to thank those at the MIT Press who helped make this book possible—particularly Doug Sery. Our thanks also go to the anonymous reviewers who provided valuable comments at the request of the MIT Press.

Timeline

When someone creates a computer artifact like a video game, a digital artwork, or a work of electronic literature, what type of process is this? Here's one idea: it is a creative act that is similar in many ways to writing a poem or taking a photograph, except that in this case, the creator doesn't use words one after another on paper or light bent through an aperture. This type of inscription or exposure doesn't happen—so what exactly does happen?

The creator of a computer work might design circuits and solder chips. Or, this author might write instructions for the integrated circuits and microprocessors of a particular computer, or write software in a high-level programming language, or create 3D models to be added to a virtual world, or edit digital video for embedding in a Web site.

The same question could be asked of the critic who interacts with such a work. What does a creator, historian, researcher, student, or other user do when experiencing a creative computer artifact? An encounter with such a work could involve trying to understand the social and cultural contexts in which it came to exist. It might also involve interpreting its representational qualities—what it means and how it produces that meaning. Alternatively, a study might involve looking at the methods of this work's construction, or the code itself, or even the hardware and physical form of the machines on which it is used.

All of these levels of computational creativity are connected. Fortunately for those of us who are interested in such uses of the computer, there have already been many studies of digital media dealing with the reception and operation of computer programs, with their interfaces, and with their forms and functions. But studies have seldom delved into the code of these programs, and they have almost never investigated the platforms that are the basis of creative computing.[1] Serious and in-depth consideration of circuits, chips, peripherals, and how they are integrated and used is a largely unexplored territory for both critic and creator.

Platforms have been around for decades, though, right underneath our video games, digital art, electronic literature, and other forms of expressive computing. Digital media researchers are starting to see that code is a way to learn more about how computers are used in culture, but there have been few attempts to go even deeper, to investigate the basic hardware and software systems upon which programming takes place, the ones that are the foundation for computational expression. This book begins to do this—to develop a critical approach to computational platforms.

We hope this will be one of several considerations of this low level of digital media, part of a family of approaches called "platform studies." Studies in this field will, we hope, investigate the relationships between platforms—the hardware and software design of standardized computing systems—and influential creative works that have been produced on those platforms.

Types of Platforms

The Atari Video Computer System (or VCS, a system also known by its product number, 2600) is a well-defined example of a platform. A platform in its purest form is an abstraction, a particular standard or specification before any particular implementation of it. To be used by people and to take part in our culture directly, a platform must take material form, as the Atari VCS certainly did. This can be done by means of the chips, boards, peripherals, controllers, and other components that make up the hardware of a physical computer system. The platforms that are most clearly encapsulated are those that are sold as a complete hardware system in a packaged form, ready to accept media such as cartridges. The Atari VCS is a very simple, elegant, and influential platform of this sort.

In other cases, a platform includes an operating system. It is often useful to think of a programming language or environment on top of an operating system as a platform, too. Whatever the programmer takes for granted when developing, and whatever, from another side, the user is required to have working in order to use particular software, is the platform. In general, platforms are layered—from hardware through operating system and into other software layers—and they relate to modular components, such as optional controllers and cards. Studies in computer science and engineering have addressed the question of how platforms are best developed and what is best encapsulated in the platform. Studies in digital media have addressed the cultural relevance of particular software that runs on platforms. But little work has been done on how the hardware and software of platforms influences, facilitates, or constrains particular forms of computational expression.

When digital media creators choose a platform, they simplify development and delivery in many ways. For example, such authors need not construct an entirely new computer system before starting on a particular creative project. Likewise, users need not fashion or acquire completely new pieces of hardware before interacting with such a work. That said, work that is built for a platform is supported and constrained by what the chosen platform can do. Sometimes the influence is obvious: a monochrome platform can't display color, for instance, and a videogame console without a keyboard can't accept typed input. But there are more subtle ways that platforms influence creative production, due to the idioms of programming that a language supports or due to transistor-level decisions made in video and audio hardware. In addition to allowing certain developments and precluding others, platforms also function in more subtle ways to encourage and discourage different sorts of computer expression. In drawing raster graphics, there is a considerable difference between setting up one television scan line at a time as the Atari VCS demands, having a buffered display with support for tiles and sprites, or having some more elaborate system that includes a native 3D renderer. Such a difference can end up being much more important than simple statistics of screen resolution or color depth that are used as shorthand by fans and marketers.

We offer here such a platform study, one that considers an influential videogame system that helped introduce computing to a popular audience and to the home. Our approach is mainly informed by the history of material texts, programming, and computing systems. Other sorts of platform studies may emphasize different technical or cultural aspects, and may draw on different critical and theoretical approaches. To deal deeply with platforms and digital media, however, any study of this sort must be technically rigorous. The detailed analysis of hardware and code connects to the experience of developers who created software for a platform and users who interacted with and will interact with programs on that platform. Only the serious investigation of computing systems as specific machines can reveal the relationships between these systems and creativity, design, expression, and culture.

Although it was not the first home videogame console, the Atari VCS was the first wildly popular one. It was affordable at the time, and it offered the flexibility of interchangeable cartridges. The popularity of the Atari VCS—which was the dominant system for years and remained widely used for more than a decade—supported the creation of nearly one thousand games, many of which established techniques, mechanics, or entire genres that continue to thrive today on much more technologically advanced platforms. Although several companies fielded consoles, by 1981 the Atari VCS accounted for 75 percent of home videogame system sales.[2] Indeed, the generic term for a videogame system in the early 1980s was "an Atari." Yet, despite its undisputed place in the annals of popular culture, and despite having been the standard system for home video gaming for so many years, Atari's first cartridge-based system is an extremely curious computer.

Cost concerns led to a remarkable hardware design, which influenced how software was written for the Atari VCS, which in turn influenced the video games created during and after the system's reign. Given that it used a version of the very typical 6502 processor, which drove many computers and consoles, one might not guess that the Atari VCS was so atypical. But this processor interfaced with the display by means of a truly unique component, the Television Interface Adaptor, or TIA. A television picture is composed of many horizontal lines, illuminated by an electron beam that traces each one by moving across and down a picture tube. Some programmers worry about having each frame of the picture ready to be displayed on time; VCS programmers must make sure that each individual *line* of each frame is ready as the electron gun starts to light it up, "racing the beam" as it travels down the screen.

The Roots of Video Gaming

In *World of Warcraft*, you start off, as a human, in Northshire Abbey. You can move your character around using the W, A, S, and D keys, an interface popularized by the first-person shooter *Quake*. As you do this, the terrain that you're standing on moves off the screen and new terrain appears as if from off screen. You are in a virtual space that is larger than the screen. This shouldn't be at all surprising. It seems that every 3D game, from *Grand Theft Auto: San Andreas* and *Super Mario 64* to *Tomb Raider*, offers virtual spaces that are larger than the screen. *Quake* and other first-person shooters have them as well, as do 2D games. In the original *Legend of Zelda*, for instance, when you have Link walk off one side of the screen, he appears on the other side of a new screen in another part of the large virtual space.

Video games weren't born with these extra-large virtual spaces, though. *Pong*, *Spacewar*, *Space Invaders*, and *Asteroids* are a few of the many games that have a single screen as their playing field. The idea of a game with a virtual space bigger than the screen had to be developed and implemented for the first time at some point.[3] This was done by Warren Robinett, as he designed and programmed *Adventure*, the first graphical adventure game, for the Atari VCS in 1978.

Engage with *Half-Life 2* and you could find your avatar, Gordon Freeman, surrounded by attacking enemies who provide supporting fire for each other, dodge, and hide behind cover, powered as they are by what the game industry calls *artificial intelligence*, or AI. The pleasure of many solo games, whether they are real-time strategy games such as *Warcraft III: Reign of Chaos* or first-person shooters, comes from the worthy but surmountable challenge that computer opponents are able to provide.

The computer's ability to play against a person and to play somewhat like a person, rather than just serving as the playing field and referee, wasn't a given in the early days of gaming. Early on, most games were either two-player, like *Pong* and *Spacewar*, or else offered an asymmetric challenge, like that of *Space Invaders*. But there were other developments that helped the industry move toward today's crafty computer-controlled enemies. One early example was Alan Miller's Atari cartridge *Basketball*, which, in its 2K of code and graphics, managed to provide a computer-controlled opponent for a one-on-one game. But even before then, one of the VCS launch titles, *Video Olympics*, offered a one-player "Robot Pong" mode that provided an opponent who, although not anthropomorphic, managed to be challenging without being impossible to defeat.

It's obvious to any gamer today, and certainly also to those who produce games, that there are well-established videogame genres: first-person shooters, real-time strategy games, sports games, driving games, platformers, adventure games, and survival horror games, for instance. Video gaming wasn't always stratified in this way. From the very early days, in which two-player head-to-head challenges predominated, video games began to branch out as games employed many types of hardware and software interfaces, display technologies, game forms, and representations. Gradually, conventions of different sorts began to emerge and various genres became evident.

Some of the development of today's videogame genres arose thanks to computer games and arcade games, but games for the Atari VCS made important contributions as well. Certain genres the Atari VCS helped develop (such as the vertical scroller, which was fostered by Activision's *River Raid*) do not define important sectors of today's videogame market. Others remain influential, such as the graphical adventure game, the prototype of which was Atari's *Adventure*, and the platformer, pioneered in Activision's *Pitfall!* One game critic even traces the origin of survival horror to the 1982 VCS cartridge *Haunted House*.[4] Regardless of whether the case for this lineage is persuasive, it is obvious that the Atari VCS was at least a seedbed for videogame genres, if not the forge in which many were formed.

The Atari VCS is certainly a retro fetish object and a focus of nostalgia, but it is also much more than this. The system is essential to the history of video games, and in niches it remains a living part of the modern videogame ecology.

Cartridge Games for the Home

The Atari Video Computer System was the first successful cartridge-based videogame console. (In 1982, when the Atari 5200 was introduced, the system was renamed the Atari 2600, the new name being taken from the system's original product number. Because our focus in this book is on the period 1977–1983, we have decided to call the console "the Atari VCS" throughout the book.) The system appeared at a time when the vast majority of video games were played in bars, lounges, and arcades. The arcade cabinet has become a rare sight in the United States, but in their best year, coin-operated games collected quarters that, adjusting for inflation, sum to more than twice the 2006 sales of U.S. computer and videogame software.[5]

Arcade games derive directly from tavern and lounge games such as pinball. They are indirectly descended from games of chance, including midway games and slot machines. Among his many trades, Atari founder Nolan Bushnell worked the midway as a barker before founding Atari.[6] His contributions to video games owe much to the principles he learned from his experiences at the carnival.

Midway games rely on partial reinforcement—a type of operant conditioning that explains how people become attached (and possibly addicted) to experiences. Partial reinforcement provides rewards at scheduled intervals. Psychologists Geoffrey R. Loftus and Elizabeth F. Loftus make the argument that video games offer superlative examples of partial reinforcement, presenting incentives at just the right moments to encourage players to continue or try again when they fail.[7]

The classic midway games, which involve things like throwing a ball into a basket or knocking down bottles, appear to be contests of skill. But the barker can subtly alter the games to tip the odds in or out of his favor. For example, by slightly, imperceptibly turning the angle of the basket, the basketball game operator can almost ensure failure, or make success very easy, for a particular throw.

Midway games are illusions more than tests of skill, designed to offer the player just enough positive feedback to give the impression that winning is easy, or at least possible. The midway barker must occasionally allow players to win, persuading onlookers and passersby that the game is a sure thing. Bushnell was a natural barker; he had an uncanny ability to read people and play to their weaknesses. He knew that the big, brutish fellow would be willing to drop a small fortune trying to beat a game that he'd just seen a weakling master.

It was as if Bushnell had all of this in mind already when he first started working with video games. As an electrical engineer educated at the University of Utah, he discovered *Spacewar* at school in 1962. That game ran on the PDP-1 minicomputer and displayed simple graphics on an oscilloscope. Steve Russell, an MIT student, had created *Spacewar* earlier that year. The game quickly spread to the few institutions fortunate enough to have a PDP-1. Given the price tag of more than $100,000, these were usually universities and laboratories.

Bushnell spent the next decade trying to make a version of *Spacewar* simple enough to run on more common, less expensive hardware. The result was *Computer Space*, which arcade game manufacturer Nutting Associates released in 1971 to very limited commercial success. Complexity of play was part of the problem—the general public wasn't accustomed to arcade games. Parlor and midway games inspire play based partly on familiarity and partly on external rewards. To make a breakthrough, Bushnell needed to merge his experience as an electrical engineer and as a midway barker.

Slot machines certainly implement the midway barker's technique, providing scheduled payouts of varying amounts based on complex odds tables. These tables were originally encoded mechanically and are now represented electronically. But pinball machines and video games give the player partial control over an experience, and in that respect they have more in common with midway games than with slot machines. In the taverns that first hosted Bushnell and Al Alcorn's coin-operated *Pong* (1972), the game became a social hub, serving a function that darts, pinball, and related tavern sports had fulfilled in that space. In *Pong* and its siblings, partial reinforcement operates on two registers. First, the game encourages continued play and rematches—it promotes "coin drop," a measure of the rate at which a machine takes in cash.[8] Second, the game encourages players to remain in the bar, ordering more food and drink. It is important to the history of video games that they bring their persuasive powers to bear within specific architectural spaces, enticing players to enter and remain within certain places.

As tavern culture gave way to the video arcade of the late 1970s and early 1980s, secondary pursuits like eating food surrendered to the primary pursuit of playing games. Arcades had more in common with casinos than with taverns. Bushnell, ever the entrepreneur, recognized this as a market opportunity and decided to create an arcade space with the additional social and gastronomical goals of a tavern, one that would also appeal to a broader audience. While still at Atari, he hatched the idea for Chuck E. Cheese's Pizza Time Theatres, a place for kids and families to eat pizza and play games.[9] Here, Bushnell combined all of his prior influences. Chuck E. Cheese's was an arcade: its games encouraged continued play and cross-cabinet play. It was also a restaurant: food and drink drew players to the locale and kept them there longer. Finally, it was a midway: players collected tickets from games of skill and chance like skeeball in the hopes of exchanging them for prizes.

Yet despite Bushnell's very relevant background, *Pong* was not simply and directly the result of one man's midway job. In 1958, Willy Higinbotham created a playable version of tennis that ran on an analog computer, with display output to an oscilloscope, just as *Spacewar* would do half a decade later. Higinbotham worked at the Brookhaven National Laboratory, a federal nuclear physics research facility on Long Island. His game, dubbed *Tennis for Two*, was created as a demo for the lab's annual visitors' day. Higinbotham intended it both as a distraction from the rather mundane operation of the facility and, purportedly, as evidence of the future potential for nuclear power.

While Bushnell was working on his tavern-grade adaptation of *Spacewar*, Ralph Baer commenced work on his television gaming device, the "Brown Box." Like Bushnell, Baer saw the potential for computer games among a broader market, but his great equalizer of choice was the television, not the tavern. The Brown Box was eventually commercialized in 1972 as the Magnavox Odyssey, the first home videogame console. Baer, a fervent supporter of patents and intellectual property protection for software and electronics, worked with Magnavox to battle successor technologies in court throughout the 1970s and 1980s in many lawsuits, some of which named Bushnell and Atari as defendants. Some of the claims against Atari rested on the similarity of *Pong* to the Odyssey's tennis game, which Bushnell had seen before *Pong* was built. Magnavox prevailed. Baer's opposition to similar-looking work seems somewhat ironic, though, given the similarity between the Brown Box's television tennis game and Higinbotham's *Tennis for Two*.[10]

Legal disputes aside, Baer and Bushnell were alike in focusing on one important component in their efforts to create consumer-affordable video games: the television. The Odyssey very obviously relied on the tube in a user's own den or living room, but the arcade game *Pong* was television-based as well, even though most of the TV was hidden away. Al Alcorn, the engineer who built *Pong*, purchased an ordinary consumer-grade black-and-white television for the cabinet, paying much less than he would have for the equivalent industrial monitor.[11]

The first *Pong* unit was installed in Andy Capp's Tavern, a bar in Sunnyvale, California. Increasingly apocryphal stories of the game's installation report lines out the door but almost never mention the precedent for coin-operated video games in Andy Capp's. When Alcorn installed *Pong* in the summer of 1972, *Computer Space* was sitting there in the bar already.[12]

Pong solved the problem that plagued *Computer Space*—ease of use—partly by being based on the familiar game table tennis and partly thanks to the simplicity of its gameplay instructions. "Avoid missing ball for high score" was a single sentence clear enough to encourage pick-up play, but vague enough to create the partial reinforcement of the slot machine and the midway; after failing, players wanted to try again. One other important sentence appeared on the machine: "Insert coin."

Pong's start in a Silicon Valley tavern rather than a corner convenience store or shopping mall is an important detail of the medium's evolution. Bars are social spaces, and the context for multiplayer games had already been set by the long tradition of darts, pool, and other games common to the tavern. *Pong* was launched in 1972; volume production of the machine started the next year; and, by 1974, there were 100,000 *Pong*-style machines that, as Martin Campbell-Kelly explained, "largely displaced pinball machines, diverting the flow of coins from an old technology to a newer one without much increasing the overall take."[13] But taverns are also adult spaces that are fewer in kind and number than the millions of living rooms and dens that had access to video games thanks to Baer and Magnavox. At a time when coin-ops ruled the market, part of the appeal of the home console system was its promise to tap into a new market of kids and families.

In 1973, just a year after *Pong*'s coin-op release, Atari started eyeing the home market for video games. The company's home version of *Pong*

1.1 To play Atari's *Home Pong*, the two players each use one of the knobs to control a paddle that appears on the TV screen.

(figure 1.1) boasted considerable technical advances over the Odyssey, including an integrated circuit that contained most of the game's logic on a single chip, on-screen scoring, and digital sound. The device connected to the television directly, but was small enough to store out of the way when not in use. Atari agreed to let Sears sell it exclusively, and the department store initially ordered 150,000 units.[14] Atari's triumph was short-lived, however. In 1976, General Instrument released its $5 AY-3-8500, a "Pong-on-a-chip" that also contained simple shooting games. This component allowed even companies without much electronics experience to bring *Pong*-like games to market, and many did just that. Campbell-Kelly writes that there were seventy-five *Pong*-like products available by the end of 1976, "being produced in the millions for a few dollars apiece."[15]

Even if Atari had cornered the market for home *Pong*, owning the system wouldn't have done anything to directly influence future purchases. Try as Atari did to enhance their product, offering new features and more controllers for multiplayer action in later versions, how many *Pong* units could one house have needed? Those at Atari therefore sought to imitate some features of the nascent personal computer with a home console that used interchangeable cartridges, allowing the system to play many games. There would be an important difference from home computing, though: all of the cartridges for the system would be made by one company.

The tremendous success of *Pong* and the home *Pong* units suggested that Atari should produce a machine capable of playing many games that were similar to *Pong*. The additional success of *Tank* by Kee Games (a pseudo-competitor that Atari CEO Bushnell created to work around the exclusivity that distributors demanded) suggested another similar game that the cartridge-based system should be capable of playing. *Tank* featured two player objects, each controllable by a separate human player, along with projectiles that bounced off walls. The computational model and basic game form were almost identical to those of *Pong*, and became the essence of *Combat*, the title that was included with the original VCS package. The simple elements present in these early games would be the basis for the console's capabilities from that point on.

Previous attempts at home machines that used interchangeable cartridges, such as the Magnavox Odyssey and the Fairchild Video Entertainment System (VES)/Channel F, brought to light some potential benefits and risks for such a system. Baer's Odyssey, released in 1972, played twelve games, but the players of these games had to attach plastic overlays to the screen to provide the sort of background that would later be accomplished with computer graphics. The machine had no memory or processor. Although the experience of playing the Odyssey was certainly that of a video game, and was important in fostering the market for home video games, the system was perhaps too simplified, even for the time. Playing it may have seemed closer to board game play with a television supplement than to later video gaming. (The inclusion of play money and dice with the system couldn't have helped in this regard.) From the release of the Odyssey in 1972 until it was discontinued in 1975, it seems that between 200,000 and 350,000 units were sold.[16] The machine introduced home videogame systems to the world, but not on the scale that the Atari VCS would, beginning in the late 1970s.

Fairchild's VES, released in 1976, was the first programmable, interchangeable cartridge system. It sported an onboard processor and random-access memory (RAM). The system had a rapid name change when Atari's VCS was released, and is better known today as the Fairchild Channel F. Even before Fairchild's system was market-tested, though, Warner Communications purchased Atari. The purchase was motivated primarily by the commercial promise of an extensible home console.[17] This 1976 acquisition provided the capital that Atari needed to bring the Atari VCS to market.

Design of the Atari VCS

The engineers developing the Atari VCS needed to account for two goals— the ability to imitate existing successful games and some amount of versatility—as they designed the circuitry for a special-purpose microcomputer for video games. Material factors certainly influenced the design. At one extreme was the high cost of hardware components. The Channel F was manufactured by Fairchild Semiconductor, and unsurprisingly the system used that company's Fairchild F8 CPU, a specialty processor created by future Intel founder Robert Noyce. At the other extreme was a lack of flexibility. The Odyssey's games were implemented directly in diode-transfer logic (DTL) on the console's circuit board. The cartridges for the Odyssey, unlike those for the Fairchild system, simply selected a game from a set of hard options.[18] The Atari VCS would need to navigate between the Scylla of powerful but expensive processors and the Charybdis of a cut-rate but inflexible set of hardwired games.

It could be done. In 1975, MOS Technology had released a new processor—the 6502. At the time, the chip was the cheapest CPU on the market by far, and it was also faster than competing chips like the Motorola 6800 and the Intel 8080.[19] The 6502's low cost and high performance made it an immensely popular processor for more than a decade. The chip drove the Apple I and Apple][, the Commodore PET and Commodore 64, the Atari 400 and 800 home computers, and the Nintendo Entertainment System (NES). It is still used today in some embedded systems.

This chip seemed attractive, as cost was the primary consideration in the design of the Atari VCS. The system needed to be much more affordable than a personal computer, which was still a very rare and expensive commodity. When Apple Computer released the popular Apple][in 1977, it cost $1,298, even after Steve Wozniak's many cost- and component-saving engineering tricks. The same year, Atari released the VCS for $199.[20] The price was just above the console's manufacturing cost, a common strategy today but an unusual one in the 1970s. Atari was betting heavily on profiting from cartridge sales, as it indeed would do.

In 1975 Atari acquired Cyan Engineering, a consulting firm.[21] Cyan's chiefs, Steve Mayer and Ron Milner, were the ones who selected the MOS 6507 for the VCS project. This chip was a stripped-down version of the already inexpensive 6502. From a programmer's perspective, the 6507 behaves more or less identically to a 6502, but it cannot address as much memory, a limitation that ended up affecting the maximum capacity of videogame cartridges for the system.

The 6507 was available for less than $25; similarly capable Intel and Motorola chips went for $200.[22] But the 6507 CPU was only one component—the Atari VCS still needed additional silicon for memory, input, graphics, and sound. The CPU does the essential arithmetic at the core of computation, but a videogame system also needs to carry out other functions; among them, the important job of producing sound and graphics. At the time, computer graphics were mostly managed in read-only memory (ROM). Character sets and video memory for a grid of rows and lines of text were reserved in a special space in ROM chips on the motherboard. Such was the case for the Tandy TRS-80 and Commodore PET, both also released in 1977. The Apple][′s graphics and sound system was implemented in a similar but more sophisticated way, thanks in part to Steve Wozniak's experience designing an Atari arcade game. As Wozniak explained:

A lot of features of the Apple][went in because I had designed *Breakout* for Atari. I had designed it in hardware. I wanted to write it in software now. So that was the reason that color was added in first—so that games could be programmed. I sat down one night and tried to put it into BASIC. Fortunately I had written the BASIC myself, so I just burned some new ROMs with line drawing commands, color changing commands, and various BASIC commands that would plot in color. I got this ball bouncing around, and I said, "Well it needs sound," and I had to add a speaker to the Apple][. It wasn't planned, it was just accidental.[23]

Wozniak engineered capabilities into ROM, burning what he needed onto chips that went onto the motherboard. Each additional chip meant more cost—exactly the luxury that the ultra-low-cost Atari VCS couldn't afford.

The Atari VCS needed a system for graphics and sound similar in principle to Wozniak's flexible Apple][, but simpler in its design and having less of an impact on hardware costs. For this purpose, the Atari VCS used a custom chip, the Television Interface Adaptor (TIA). Joe Decuir and Jay Miner designed the TIA, which was code-named "Stella"— a name also used for the machine as a whole, and one which came from the brand of Decuir's bicycle.[24] Of course, the two sought to simplify the hardware design as much as possible, reducing its complexity and cost. For this reason, a custom graphics chip was the only real option. The cost of TIA research and development must have far outweighed any other development cost for the system, and yet it was a wise investment, given that graphics and sound are so essential to video games.

RAM, the memory programs use to store temporary information while they are running, was very expensive at the time, so an important cost-saving measure was limiting its use. In 1977, the Apple][shipped with 4K of RAM. The TRS-80 and PET, both shipped in that same year, also sported 4K. In 1982, the Commodore 64 shipped with 64K, the maximum amount addressable by the 6502. By contrast, the Atari VCS has only 128 *bytes* of RAM. That amount is $\frac{1}{32}$ of that in general-purpose microcomputers of the late 1970s and not enough to store this ASCII-encoded sentence. RAM remained a costly prospect through the 1980s, and many home game consoles scrimped on it to reduce costs. The 128-byte memory of the VCS was twice as large as the standard RAM of the Channel F. The significantly more advanced NES had sixteen times as much RAM at 2K.

In addition to the processor, the graphics system, and memory, the fourth major component of the system, a chip called the Peripheral Interface Adaptor (PIA) or RAM/Input/Output/Timer (RIOT), handles input from the two player controls and the console switches. Unlike the Odyssey, the Channel F, and a competitor that was to arrive in 1979 (the Intellivision), the VCS let players plug in different controllers right out of the box. Two different kinds were included with the system, and several different styles were marketed by Atari and third parties during the console's long commercial life. Most notably, though, the Atari VCS introduced the joystick to the home videogame player as the standard control.

In studying the Atari VCS from the perspective of the platform, several things stand out about the system and its influence on the future of video games. One is the strong relationship between the console and the television. Baer correctly predicted that the TV would be central to video games. (Games driven by computer power had previously been designed for less common displays, such as oscilloscopes, or crafted for use on print or video terminals.) The Atari VCS—particularly its graphics and sound chip, the TIA—is designed to interface solely (and weirdly) with a standard CRT television, the sort common in living rooms and dens of the 1970s. Its controllers and peripherals were fashioned for use on the floor or the couch. The games made for the platform are likewise oriented toward home use—either for enjoying the arcade experience at home or for playing in different ways with friends and family. The focus on the production of images for display on the TV helps explain why games running on circuits and later computers became known as "video games."

Another strong current in the work on the Atari VCS is the powerful influence of earlier games. Many—perhaps most—VCS cartridges are to a greater or lesser extent ports of arcade games. The system's architecture was designed with the popular coin-op games *Pong* and *Tank* in mind. Many early VCS titles were directly ported from coin-op games. Even very innovative titles like *Adventure* were directly inspired by games on other computer systems. After 1980, licensed arcade and film adaptations became popular as well, especially at Warner-owned Atari. But beyond ports of coin-op games and adaptations from other entertainment media, the 1977–1983 era was one of uncertainty and experimentation in video games. Nobody really knew what would make a good subject for a game, and many relied on previous successes. Atari's liberal use of the term "video" in game titles underscores the company's reliance on transforming familiar subjects into games for play on a television: *Video Olympics*, *Video Checkers*, *Video Cube*.

A final observation is the tremendous representational flexibility of the machine and the less-than-obvious reason for this flexibility. The games created for the platform during its long life cover innumerable subjects and situations: dogfighting, bridge, hockey, treasure hunting, lassoing, slot car racing, dental care, and even sex acts. The breadth of the system's software library becomes even more striking when one considers that two simple arcade games were the major inspirations for its hardware design—and that no one fathomed how successful and long-lived the console would be.

So much was possible on the Atari VCS, and not because it was a powerful computer. It wasn't powerful at all. Rather, so much was possible because the machine was so simple. The very few things it could do well—drawing a few movable objects on the screen one line at a time while uttering sounds using square waves and noise—could be put together in a wide variety of ways to achieve surprising results.

Plan of the Book

In this book we concentrate on six VCS cartridges while also discussing many others along the way.[25] We selected these six cartridges from the many hundreds that have been developed because they particularly enlighten the discussion of the VCS platform and creative production upon it. We discuss them in chronological order, so that the development of programming practices and the changes in home and arcade video gaming can be tracked more easily through time. The cartridges that are central to our discussion are as follows:

• *Combat*, the cartridge that was originally bundled with the Atari VCS. This set of two-player tank and plane games demonstrates almost all of the basic hardware capabilities of the system in a straightforward way. It also reveals a great deal about the relationship of home video gaming to arcade games, showing how even the first home games based on arcade games would use them as a starting point and often transform them.

• *Adventure*, which established the action-adventure genre. This game represents a virtual space that is larger than the screen, showing how some of the affordances of the VCS platform can be used for purposes that were different than those originally intended. *Adventure* was also a radically different adaptation of an all-text computer game, one that again helps to reveal the influence of platforms in creative production.

• *Pac-Man*, a more direct take on a successful arcade game—one that spawned a massive craze, or, one might say, a fever. The cartridge was widely derided as being a poor, inauthentic port of the arcade game, yet it nevertheless became the overall best-selling cartridge for the Atari VCS. The mismatch between the arcade *Pac-Man* and the capabilities of the VCS hardware is particularly revealing.

• *Yars' Revenge*, Atari's best-selling original VCS game. Even this "original" started as a conversion of an arcade title. The conversion was jettisoned and a highly complex game took shape, one with unique graphics that was well-suited to home play. This cartridge shows another important way in which some arcade platforms (those using a fundamentally different display technology, *vector* or *XY* graphics) differed from the Atari VCS. It also reveals how a programmer used his knowledge of the VCS hardware to fashion a novel and effective game rather than implementing a partial and ineffective re-creation. The cartridge *Asteroids*, a contemporary of *Yars' Revenge*, is discussed in some detail as another case of a vector graphics game being adapted to the Atari VCS.

• *Pitfall!*, another innovative original that was developed at Activision, the first third-party videogame company. This game helps to show the difference between cartridges produced by Activision and those produced by Atari for the same platform, and it also provides a way to look at the rise of third-party videogame companies and the platform-related challenges they faced. *Pitfall!* was also a critical step in the development of the action-adventure genre and an important step toward the side scroller.

• *Star Wars: The Empire Strikes Back*, probably the most unusual choice of these six. Obviously, it is a game that was produced under license and was meant to exploit the success of a popular film. Although not the most famous VCS game of this sort, *Star Wars: The Empire Strikes Back* shows how a compelling cinematic situation can be translated effectively into a videogame challenge. The cartridge also provides a good opportunity to discuss the explosion of third-party titles and the interaction between media properties and video games, along with the collapse of the Atari VCS market that ensued in 1983. Finally, it reveals how much the use of the VCS platform had escaped from the proprietary hold of Atari and how much it had advanced during the time period we are considering.

The book concludes with a short chapter. Although our platform study focuses on the Atari VCS during 1977–1983, this final chapter briefly considers some of the high points of the life of the Atari VCS from 1983 to the present, discussing what else has been learned about the platform and how this platform has interacted with culture during this span of time. Finally, in an afterword, we look ahead to see what other platforms, and what other issues, can be addressed by future platform studies, and to consider what insights this approach can offer as we continue to think about creative digital media.

The Atari VCS console was given the model number CX2600 and was sold with two joystick controllers, two paddle controllers, a TV/game radio frequency switch box, and a cartridge bearing the product number that came next in sequence, CX2601. This cartridge was *Combat*, a "game program" with twenty-seven games, according to the included manual: variants of Tank, Tank-Pong, Invisible Tank, Invisible Tank-Pong, Biplane, and Jet. The button fires a missile in all of the games. In the tank games, moving a joystick left or right turns an iconic tank; moving a joystick up causes the tank that it is controlling to go forward. Obstacles are present in some of the tank games, and there are other variations in play, such as rebounding shots and invisibility. The two plane games are similar to the tank ones, but there are no obstacles in any of them—only blocky, obscuring clouds in some variants—and the planes always move forward. The way the planes are controlled is different, too. The player whose tank or plane has been hit fewer times at the end of a game, which lasts two minutes and sixteen seconds, is the winner.

    Combat was programmed while the Atari VCS hardware was being developed, growing from a tank game that was part of the concept prototype for the system. In many ways, the cartridge and the system were designed for one another. *Combat* is practically a pure demonstration of the capabilities of the Atari VCS, showing how they were intended to be used: the VCS stripped bare by its bachelors. The joysticks control the two player sprites, while each player fires a missile represented by one of two built-in missile sprites. The more blocky background part of the image—

actually a foreground of cloud cover in the plane games and a maze structure in the tank games—is both horizontally and vertically symmetrical in all of the games. This lower-resolution part of the screen is called the "playfield." The horizontal symmetry is accomplished in a very straightforward way, by setting a particular bit. One of the few facilities not used is the ball sprite, an element provided for *Pong*-like games, in which a single ball is bounced back and forth between players. Although it did not use the ball, *Combat* did use *Pong*-like logic to allow the missiles to rebound in the Tank-Pong games.

Although the Atari VCS was not sold until October 1977, something like *Combat* existed in an early form by late 1975. Steve Mayer had written a tank game for an early version of the VCS hardware, a prototype that was designed by Ron Milner. Joe Decuir joined the VCS team that December and helped debug this proto-*Combat*. In March of the next year, he moved to a different office to apprentice for Jay Miner. Decuir rewrote the tank game while working with Miner to design the VCS chipset. The core of the program had been finished by that point, but the cartridge was made into its final form by Larry Wagner, who was the lead cartridge programmer for *Combat*. Wagner refined the tank games and added both sorts of plane games.

Although it was the first cartridge for the Atari VCS, *Combat*—like so many video games on this system and other platforms—was not truly original. The basis for *Combat*'s tank games was the successful arcade game *Tank*, released in November 1974. *Tank* was marketed by Kee Games, a purported competitor to Atari that was actually wholly owned by the company and run by Joe Keenan, Nolan Bushnell's friend and next-door neighbor. Kee Games was established to make the videogame industry look bigger—to make it seem that Atari was not the only company involved with arcade video games, and also to skirt certain regulatory hurdles of the coin-op business.[1] After the ruse was discovered, Atari offered Keenan a job as president. He accepted and became an effective leader of the rapidly growing company.

Tank was remarkable both as the biggest hit from Kee Games and because it pioneered the use of ROM chips in video games. The nature of ROM was important to the Atari VCS, and ROM is a reasonable starting point for technical discussion, so it is worthwhile to look into the technology and its use in video gaming in some depth.

The Use of ROM in Video Games

"ROM" is a generic term for any memory that can be easily read, but cannot be written to, or can be rewritten only with difficulty. There are

ROM technologies that are not truly "read-only." Programmable read-only memory (PROM) can be burned in the field rather than in the factory, for instance, and Flash ROM, commonly used in today's consumer electronics, including cameras and routers, can be rewritten—although not rapidly. In the broadest sense, though, ROM is still much more difficult to write than to read. Unlike random-access memory (RAM), all types of ROM are also nonvolatile, so ROM does not have to remain powered to keep its contents.

Atari's driving game *Gran Trak 10* was the very first to have a store of ROM, but it did not use a chip to implement this memory. It stored sprite graphics in a matrix of diodes, each of which was placed individually on the printed circuit board. This was a costly way to store data, and required more space on the board than a single chip would. It was groundbreaking to use ROM of any sort, but this particular technique was not the way forward for arcade or home video games. The important ROM technology for gaming and other computing applications was *mask ROM*, in which the whole memory was stored on a single chip. This was the technology introduced in *Tank*. It was also the technology used to create the ROM chips that were the central components of *Combat* cartridges and of every other standard VCS cartridge.

A mask ROM, the classic type of ROM and one that is still in use today, is a memory that is hardwired at the time of manufacture and cannot be reflashed repeatedly or even programmed once in the field. This sort of ROM is produced like any other integrated circuit, in a lithographic process that uses a set of photomasks to etch a wafer.

Mask ROMs have high setup costs, and there is no way to make a change, however small, without incurring these costs again. The lead time is also long, with manufacturing taking several weeks. However, mask ROMs have the advantage of being very cheap to manufacture in quantity. Although they were not as flexible as other types of data storage technologies in use at the time, such as the cassette tapes that were used in home computing, mask ROMs were also more durable. A cartridge with one mask ROM on it was also cheaper to manufacture than a game board with many components on it—the alternative that the Magnavox Odyssey had previously used on that console's main board, and the way that early arcade games were put together. Generally, reusing the console's microprocessor in combination with a variety of different programs, each stored on a mask ROM, was very cost-effective, in addition to being very flexible. However difficult programming the Atari VCS was—and it was not easy—it certainly made economic sense when compared to putting together a new set of integrated circuits for each game.

In the arcade setting of the 1970s, it was not very important to be able to play multiple games with the hardware in a single cabinet. So, ROM first made its way into *Gran Trak 10*, *Tank*, and other coin-op games as a way of storing graphics data rather than programs for microprocessors. ROM was used differently on the Atari VCS: to store whole game programs, code as well as data. The system was designed to be modular and to accept different cartridges, with different programs stored in cartridge ROM. The ports that allowed the use of different controllers—either of the two types that shipped with the system as well as additional ones from Atari and other companies—were another versatile feature that offered an additional sort of modularity.

Joysticks and Other Controllers

The Atari VCS was the first cartridge-based system to come with a joystick controller. Although joysticks were already in use in arcades by 1977, the introduction of the VCS joystick into the context of the home undoubtedly did much to popularize the controller. The system's rubber-coated black controller with its one red button has become emblematic of the Atari VCS and of retro gaming, if not of video games in general. More generally, the joystick became the standard controller for home video gaming and for computer gaming. Joysticks are still important to modern console systems, although now they are thumb-scale, allow more precise movement, and find their place alongside directional pads, buttons, and triggers on the contemporary game controller.

 Combat was based on an arcade game that used joystick controllers, a game that influenced another home unit. Coleco introduced the dedicated *Telstar Combat!* system in 1977, before the VCS hit the market that year. Like *Tank*, it lacked anything resembling the Biplane and Jet games that *Combat* had. But it was certainly a close cousin of the cartridge.

 Telstar Combat! uses the General Instrument AY-3-8700 Tank chip, a follow-up to that company's AY-3-8500 Pong chip. It has four two-way joysticks—two for each player—just like *Tank*. The most successful arcade tank game, the one-player game *Battlezone*, also used a two-joystick control scheme. The two joysticks controlled the speed of the tank's two treads in *Battlezone*, however; the two joysticks per player in *Tank* determined rotation and velocity.

 The Atari VCS running *Combat*, in contrast, used two four-directional joysticks, one for each player. Even in the first VCS cartridge, designed as it was along with the Atari VCS itself, there arose the issue of the difference between the controller scheme of the inspirational arcade game and the available VCS controllers. The VCS controllers were simpler than those in many contemporary arcade games. Although it was possible to develop new controllers, the cost and difficulty of doing so precluded it in almost every case. It also wasn't tenable to produce arcade-style controls of greater durability, higher quality, and higher cost for the home market. For these reasons, VCS ports of arcade games would not, generally, be able to use exactly the same control scheme as their arcade counterparts, just as *Combat* could not use controllers that were exactly like those in *Tank*.

Along with the lack of true originality in most VCS games—that is, the basis of many VCS games in arcade games or licensed properties—another closely related theme runs throughout the history of the Atari VCS, that of the transformative port or adaptation. When an earlier game is the basis for a VCS game, it can almost never be reproduced on the VCS platform with perfect fidelity. The platforms are not the same computationally, for one thing, which is particularly important. The contexts of home play are not the same, either. The gap extends to matters of business and to the two different economic contexts. The mismatch in interface—the identical controllers are not available and input cannot be provided as it was in the earlier game—is simply one of the most visible ways in which these underlying distinctions appear.

In the tank games of *Combat*, the problem was solved by loading the rotation function and velocity function onto the same joystick, so that left and right motion rotates a tank and up causes it to move in the direction it is pointing. The button is, of course, used to fire. The plane games are generally similar, but moving the joystick up or down increases or decreases the velocity of the planes, which are never stationary.

The chip on the VCS board that handles most of the input from controllers is a standard one, a MOS Technology 6532. The 6532 provides several facilities. In addition to offering two eight-bit parallel I/O ports for controllers, it also has a programmable interval timer, a low-level programming convenience that helps to synchronize program execution with the operation of the graphics system. Finally, the 6532 contains the machine's 128 bytes of RAM. Because of these three functions, the chip is called the RIOT (RAM/Input/Output/Timer); in the *Stella Programmer's Guide*, it is referred to as the Peripheral Interface Adaptor (PIA). The 6532's 128 bytes constitute the entire store of RAM for the Atari VCS and have to be used to hold both variables, representing things like the game state and score, and the stack, which holds the program state when routines are called. The Atari VCS, like other cartridge-based systems, ran programs directly from ROM without loading them into

RAM, so RAM did not have to hold programs, as it does now and as it did on contemporary home computers.

In addition to the joysticks, the Atari VCS shipped with two paddle controllers. These are smaller than the joysticks and each features a large, round wheel that rotates through a fixed arc of roughly 330 degrees, with a stop at either end. Each paddle also includes a red button on one side. Paddle controllers (figure 2.1) are typically used to control a game object that needs to move along only one axis, such as the bat in *Pong* and *Break-out*. The positions of the paddle controllers, determined with the potentiometers inside, are read using a different and very important chip, the TIA (Television Interface Adaptor), which is discussed in much more detail later in this chapter. The paddle triggers, along with other controller data, are read using the PIA. The settings of the console switches (select, reset, color/black-and-white, and left and right difficulty) are also read from the same component.

VCS controllers function in a very straightforward way. A particular byte in memory represents the state of both joysticks. The left player's joystick state updates bits 4, 5, 6, 7, corresponding to up, down, left, and right. Bits 0, 1, 2, and 3 map to the state of the right player's joystick. This

2.1   The Atari VCS paddle controllers work by measuring output from an internal potentiometer. Atari also released a driving controller for use with *Indy 500*. It has almost the same appearance, but its knob rotates freely, rather than stopping at the extreme left and right.

allows for bits 4 (left player, up) and 7 (left player, right) to both be 1, so that diagonal positions can be read and movement in a total of eight directions is possible.

A few additional aspects of *Combat*'s controls are worth noting. Unlike the controls in dedicated home games such as the home version of *Pong* and Coleco's *Telstar Combat!*, the game's joysticks are connected by cords to the console, where they are plugged in. This means that they can be unplugged and different controllers can be swapped in for different games; it also means that players can sit back away from the main video-game unit as they play. In this regard, the Atari VCS followed the lead of the Magnavox Odyssey and the Fairchild Channel F. The availability of the joystick controller was something new, however. It can be used to rotate a simulated vehicle and to control its velocity, as in *Combat*, but its additional degree of freedom also allows for a player sprite to be intuitively moved in two dimensions, with up moving the player sprite up, right moving it right, and so on. This is the type of immediate control that helped inspire the "direct manipulation" concept of computer interfaces in the 1980s.

How the System Computes

Steve Mayer and Ron Milner began the work on the VCS project. They were chiefs at Cyan Engineering, a consulting firm that Atari purchased in 1975. An important early decision that they made involved selecting the processor that would go into the machine. They chose the ultra-low-cost MOS Technology 6507. This chip's silicon is identical to that of the more popular 6502; the package was what made it cheaper. (The package, which holds the etched section of silicon wafer and allows wires to connect to it, accounts for a significant portion of the cost of a processor.) The 6507's reduced package has fewer pins than the one for the 6502, offering only thirteen address lines. These lines are used to designate which byte in memory will be read or written. In the VCS, these lines are used to address the mask ROM in the cartridges. The thirteen lines of the 6507—compared to the 6502's sixteen address lines, which allowed that chip to address 2^{16} = 64K, an ability that home computers such as the Commodore 64 fully used—meant that the 6507 was capable of addressing only 2^{13} = 8K.

The processor selection thus constrained the system to using no more than 8K of memory at once. Given the tremendous cost of 8K mask ROMs at the time, and perhaps with the idea that many interesting games could fit in as little as 2K as *Combat* did, the designers of the Atari VCS made another choice that further constrained the system. They selected a cartridge interface that was inexpensive, and that had one fewer address line than what was provided by the processor's package. This interface left the system with the ability to address only 4K of cartridge ROM at once. Bill Gates may have thought that 640K should be enough for anybody; Mayer and Milner figured that 4K would do. This was actually a reasonable choice: a wide variety of 2K and 4K games were developed. Thanks to a technique called "bank switching" (discussed in chapters 4 and 6), larger ROMs were eventually used in VCS games.

Though central to the Atari VCS, the 6507 was only one component of several. The 6532, with its RAM, controller facilities, and timer, was another necessary part of the system. Controllers—initially, joysticks and paddles—were another. And cartridges with ROM were essential, too. These are some of the elements indicated on the block diagram of the Atari VCS architecture (figure 2.2). Another very important element appears there, but has yet to be discussed in detail: the chip that powered VCS sound and graphics.

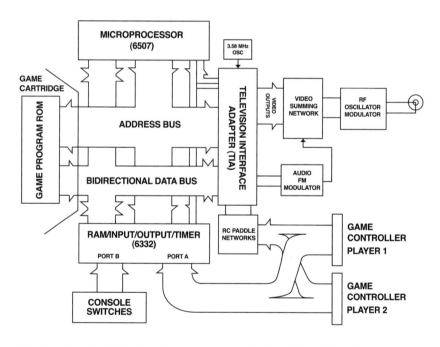

2.2 This high-level sketch of the components of the Atari VCS and how they are put together, called a "block diagram," is based on a hand-drawn one shown by Decuir in his presentation "Three Generations of Game Machine Architecture."

The processor is always called the "brain" of a computer, and, indeed, the MOS Technology 6507 is the Atari VCS's brain. But the custom Television Interface Adapter (TIA) is its heart.

For sound and graphics, functions essential to a videogame system, the Atari VCS used this chip, code-named Stella and designed from scratch by Joe Decuir and Jay Miner. The TIA makes programming a challenge, but also allows programmers to achieve a wide variety of effects with a relatively small number of individual features.

The bare-bones nature of the TIA makes seemingly basic tasks (such as drawing the game's screen) complex. An ordinary television picture of the late 1970s and early 1980s was displayed on a cathode ray tube (CRT). In a CRT, patterns of electrons are fired at glass that is coated on the inside with phosphors. These glow to create the visible picture. The screen image is not drawn all at once, but in individual scan lines, each of which is created as the electron gun slews from side to side across the screen. After each line, the beam is turned off and the gun resets its position at the start of the next line. It continues this process for as many scan lines as the TV image requires. Then it turns off again and resets to its initial position at the start of the screen. As Marshall McLuhan mused, "The scanning finger of the TV screen is at once the transcending of mechanism and a throw-back to the world of the scribe."[2]

Modern computer systems offer a facility for transcending the TV's electronic finger. They have a frame buffer, a space in memory to which the programmer can write graphics information for one entire screen draw. This facility was even provided by many systems of the late 1970s, including the Fairchild VES/Channel F, a system that made it to market before the Atari VCS. In a frame-buffered graphics system, the computer's video hardware automates the process of translating the information in memory for display on the screen, and it also manages graphical administrivia such as screen synchronization.

The VCS does not provide such services for graphics rendering. The machine is not equipped with enough memory to store an entire screen's worth of data in a frame buffer. The 128 bytes of RAM in the system are not even enough to store one eight-bit color value for every line of the 192-line visible display. There is certainly no general way to store multiple elements per line such as individual pixels, or, at a higher level, numerous moving objects, obstacles, and backgrounds. The interface between the processor and the television is also not automated, as it is in a frame-buffered graphics system.

Instead, the VCS programmer must draw each frame of a program's display manually to the screen, synchronizing the 6507 processor instructions to the television's electron gun via the TIA. The program has a small amount of time to change the TIA settings via its numerous addressable registers. This can happen when the electron beam resets to draw a new line (this period is called "horizontal blank"), or when it moves back up to the top to draw a new screen (a period called "vertical blank"). The program must also explicitly instruct the TIA to wait for the horizontal blank or to initiate the vertical blank, which involves keeping track of how much time the instructions take to execute on a single line, between lines, and between frames. Programming the Atari VCS means drawing every line of the television display individually, making decisions about how to change the display on a line-by-line basis rather than setting up a screenful of pixels all at once. This task requires that the programmer write carefully timed code that fits the motion of the television's electron beam. Some graphical effects demand changes to the TIA's registers in the middle of a single scan line. In these cases, the programmer must carefully "cycle count" processor instructions so they execute at the right time. While "racing the beam" is a catchier name, "pacing the beam" is more apt, since the program might have to be sped up or slowed down.

From the player's perspective, the Atari VCS displays its games on the two-dimensional surface of a television display. But from the machine's—and the programmer's—perspective, the television picture is a comb of horizontal lines, each section rendered on CRT phosphor with the color set at the last alteration of the TIA's registers. Consequently, there is really no such thing as a "pixel" on the Atari VCS. A pixel represents a fixed segment of a Cartesian grid, having both width and height. On the vertical axis, the smallest segment of a VCS picture is a scan line. There are 192 visible scan lines per frame on an NTSC television.[3] On the horizontal axis, the closest VCS analogue to a pixel is the smallest amount of time that can pass between changes to the electron beam's intensity as adjusted by the TIA. This is a measure of time, not of space. In the *Stella Programmer's Guide* it is referred to as a "color clock cycle" or a "color clock," a reference to the internal clock of the TIA itself.[4] The highest resolution graphics the TIA can draw are sprites, which can be as small as eight color clock cycles across (figure 2.3).

To facilitate the cycle counting mentioned earlier, the TIA is synchronized to the 6507 clock so that three TIA clock counts elapse for every machine cycle on the processor. Most 6502 instructions take three or four cycles to execute, effectively limiting the horizontal resolution possible without the use of sprite graphics. For example, simply changing the

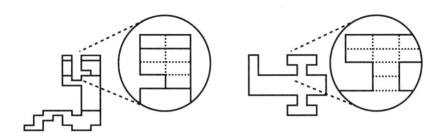

2.3   The smallest vertical unit in the VCS graphics system is a single scan line. The smallest unit of horizontal space is a color clock. The detailed view of Pitfall Harry's head and neck on the left clearly shows that the "pixel" defined by these is rectangular, not square. This shape became a design feature; for example, the rectangular blocks help Pitfall Harry's legs appear longer than they would with square pixels. The *Combat* biplane sprite on the right appears to be comprised of square pixels because that program uses a two-line kernel, which updates the sprite graphics only every two scan lines.

background color so that a part of the scan line is drawn first in one color and then in another involves storing a new value in the TIA register that holds the screen background color. A store requires three of the 6502's processor cycles to complete. (Practically, more computation has to be done to get the new color value ready. This might involve loading an eight-bit number or performing some mathematical operation that yields a new value.) Because each machine cycle corresponds to three color clock cycles, and because the instruction to store a new value in the appropriate TIA register is essential in every case, a strip of background color cannot be less than 3 processor cycles × 3 color clocks per processor cycle = 9 color clocks wide—just a bit more than the width of a sprite.

Figure 2.4 depicts a typical VCS frame, this one from *Pitfall!*, including both the visible parts of the picture and those during which the electron beam repositions itself. The first three lines are called "vertical sync." During this time, the VCS signals to the television that a new frame needs to start. The television responds by beginning to reposition the electron gun.

Next comes the "vertical blank" period, which, as mentioned earlier, represents the time it takes for the television to actually reposition the beam for the next frame. This takes as long as it does to draw 37 scan lines. During this time, the VCS program can handle game inputs and run any logic needed to set up the new frame of image and sound.

Next comes the main television picture. Each scan line of television picture is composed of a horizontal blanking period of 68 color counts, or

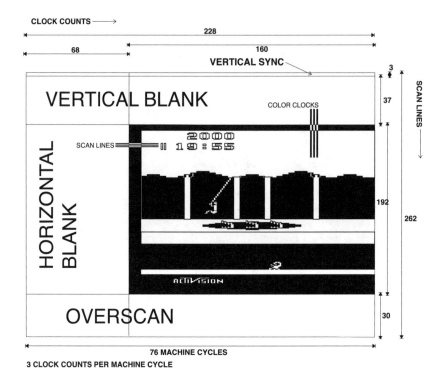

2.4 The Atari VCS television image is broken down and key regions and measures are indicated. This television protocol image is based on the one in Wright, *Stella Programmer's Guide*.

a little more than 22 machine cycles, and a visible picture period of 160 color counts, or a little more than 53 machine cycles. The numbers at the top show the clock counts and those at the bottom show the machine cycles. The short horizontal blank period is used to set up the next line of the display, for example, changing sprite and playfield graphics. If the programmer needs to make a change mid-scan line—for example, changing playfield graphics for an asymmetrical playfield—it is necessary to cycle count to insure the TIA registers change at exactly the right position in the scan line. The relative size of both a color clock and a scan line are marked in relation to the screen in figure 2.4.

Next comes the *overscan period*. At the time the Atari VCS was designed, the position of the CRT in the television casing varied considerably. The overscan period is a "safe zone" to account for this, and it provides the programmer with another thirty scan lines of time to run program logic.

Combat imitated the coin-op games *Pong* and *Tank*, and the home versions of these games, in an important way: it was a game for two players, as the cartridge label clearly stated. Instead of providing simulated opponents of some sort, as many later games would do, *Combat* offered a playing field and a means by which two players, sitting side by side, could compete against one another.

It was common for an arcade machine to provide a one-player challenge. Pinball and skeeball games did this, pitting the player against difficult terrain. Later arcade games like *Lunar Lander* and *Space Invaders* would offer a similar challenge for a single player. But another concept involved something like a table tennis setup. With this scheme, instead of having a challenging landscape to traverse or a simulated opponent with artificial intelligence, human players provide the skill and intelligence that make the game enjoyable. Very early computer and video games, such as *Tennis for Two*, *Spacewar*, the games of the Magnavox Odyssey, and *Pong*, were designed along these lines.

Of course, a single player can toy with a two-player game. A common experience among many young VCS players was that of "one-player" *Combat*, in which a single person takes one of the joysticks, goes after an inert tank or cruising plane, and pummels the unconscious enemy with repeated fire. Although such a practice does not represent the height of videogame experience, this mode of interaction does allow players to explore the different variations and learn something about how tanks and planes function in each. It also offers something to do with the title when a second human player isn't around.

A player using the left joystick and progressing through the twenty-seven games included in the *Combat* cartridge, alone or with an opponent, finds that the games vary in several significant ways. There are six game categories. Tank, the first category, has tanks firing either a straight or guided missile in one of three types of terrain. Shots do not rebound off the walls in the tank games, but they do in games in the next category, Tank-Pong. In some of these games, a "billiard hit" (a shot that rebounds at least once) is required for a kill. There are also Invisible Tank and Invisible Tank-Pong games, in which one's tank can only be seen when it fires or is hit.

The remaining categories of game are the two plane games, Biplane and Jet, which can be played with or without obscuring clouds. The biplanes, which appear in profile, climb when the joystick is pressed down and dive when the joystick is pressed up. Moving the joystick to the right causes them to gain speed (up to a point) and moving the joystick left slows them down. In addition to the straight and guided missile options, Biplane games 17 and 18 offer a different armament—machine guns. In the final category of games, the Jet games, the jets are seen from above. Up and down increases and decreases the speed of the plane, and right and left turn the plane clockwise and counterclockwise. In some Biplane and Jet games—19, 20, 25, 26, and 27—the players control multiple planes that fly in formation. There are even two asymmetrical games in which the left player has one plane (that is harder to hit) while the right player has three (that together fire more shots).

Lopsided play was supported in other ways. Although the basic framework of the videogame system was one of equality, evenness, and fairness—identical joysticks or paddles for each of the two players, symmetrical playing fields, similar-looking sprites with similar controls—the VCS designers allowed for this symmetry to be broken. The left and right difficulty switches can each be set independently to "A" (harder) or "B" (easier). In *Combat*, setting a switch to "A" decreases the range of one's fire and, if a plane game is being played, causes one's plane to fly at a slower rate. This was also in keeping with cultural norms, which require that game equipment and courts be evenhanded but allow for difficulty adjustment by "handicapping" the more advanced player—removing a pawn before play starts in a chess game, for instance, or burdening a horse with an impost that must be carried in a race. By featuring difficulty switches, the Atari VCS offered itself for use by pairs of players who might be older and younger siblings, children and parents, novice and expert.

It was sensible, given the 2K ROM size of *Combat* and the other limitations of the Atari VCS, for developers to provide a cartridge with several closely related games. The different variants use much of the same code, and the logic that is specific to each variant lets different players excel at different games. This allows people to each prefer their own favorite variants, to beat their friends at some while being much weaker at others, and to generally have more fun with the cartridge. To understand how these variants were realized in *Combat*, it is necessary to look at the code itself in more detail.

Combat's Code

Although VCS programming is an arcane practice, people today—even those with limited programming experience—can read and understand

VCS programs. Even when the machine code that is stored in a ROM is the only thing that is available, it is possible to make some sense of a VCS program through disassembly.

An *assembler* takes the instructions in an assembly language program—the source code—and converts them into the correct references for processor execution. Assembler code is nearly identical to machine code, and corresponds directly. The only difference is that the former provides convenient mnemonics and reference names for processor instructions, memory locations, registers, and so forth.

Assembler: LDA #2
Machine: A9 02

Compilers for languages like C and Java take higher-level commands and convert them into sets of machine instructions. Assemblers simply reformat processor instructions. For this reason, a VCS ROM is essentially just a copy of its source code, obfuscated by the process of assembly. A *disassembler* can be used to convert ROM instructions and data back into readable assembly language code. Code obtained in this manner does not include any natural language information labeling memory locations, or lines, or subroutines, but someone familiar with the platform, given some time, can often usefully reconstruct a program's source code using this technique.

When a program has been carefully disassembled and commented, as has been done with *Combat*, understanding the program becomes much more tractable. A thorough disassembly of the *Combat* code by Harry Dodgson, Nick Bensema, and Roger Williams—in combination with resources that are available online such as the *Stella Programmer's Guide* and *Atari 2600 Programming for Newbies*—makes it possible for the serious student of the Atari VCS to trace through the program and understand how it was put together.

Rather than trying to repeat the line-by-line analysis of code that has already been done in the *Combat* disassembly, we will outline the high-level structure of the program and zoom in on only a few telling details. In later chapters, consideration of other sections of cartridge code will continue to inform our analysis of the relationship between the VCS platform and the creative works programmed for it.

The basic flow of *Combat* follows the progress of the TV's electron beam, busily preparing each line that is to be drawn while the current one is appearing on the screen. During the vertical blanking interval, as the beam moves from the bottom of the screen to the top, the VCS running *Combat* does the computation necessary to process input, deal with game logic, and update the score if necessary.

The first routine in *Combat*'s main loop checks the position of the VCS console switches. A game can be reset at any time, so it is necessary to check these controls each frame. This routine allows different game variations to be selected—if a game is not already in progress—and, if a game is in progress, it also checks to see whether time is almost up and the score should be blinking. This routine also underscores the fact that the programmer is responsible for handling every interaction on the machine. The Atari VCS has no operating system to intercept inputs and respond to common ones. Thus, even though the reset switch is clearly labeled "reset" on the console cabinet, it is up to each cartridge programmer to write a program that responds to the switch being pressed. The programmer can choose to have a cartridge do something other than reset the game when the reset switch is closed, just as different games might use the joystick button for different actions. Although this was rare, there are examples of games that override the function of the console switches as printed on the console. One is *Space Shuttle: A Journey into Space*, discussed in chapter 6.

The next routine sets the VCS number-size registers and, if a game isn't under way, ignores joystick input and cycles the screen's colors in a simple sort of attract mode. The attract loop also serves as a screensaver, insuring that a game left unattended will not burn its image irreversibly into the phosphors of the CRT. In the routine after this, the joystick positions are checked for both tanks or planes unless one has been temporarily immobilized by being hit. After this, a lengthy routine checks for collisions between the missiles and the tanks or planes, between tank and wall, and between tank and tank. With this information determined, the position of tanks or planes can be updated in the next routine. While that routine handles the translation in space that needs to be done, another one is needed to deal with rotation. So the next routine updates the orientation of the tanks or planes and selects the correct sprite image from sixteen bytes of RAM. A complex calculation must then be done to convert the score from its internal representation as a binary-coded decimal to an offset that can be used to look up the correct ROM data to depict a numeral. Finally, after all of this is done, a routine called the "kernel" is called to draw the display by setting up the scan lines one at a time. The kernel is the last routine in *Combat*'s main loop.

Game Variations

The game's variations are stored entirely in a small lookup table of settings which the main program reads and writes to appropriate RAM locations at the start of a game. To allow for variations in sprite graphics, the TIA offers two number-size registers that enforce automatic modifications to the sprites when drawn on-screen, named $NUSIZ_0$ and $NUSIZ_1$. In particular, the programmer can change the number of sprites drawn on a single line as well as the size of the sprites. A missile graphic, which is always the same color as its parent player sprite, can also have its size adjusted. Adjustments to the sprites are made by setting one or more of the lowest three bits on the number-size register. The following table offers a summary of the size and number adjustments afforded by this register:

D_2	D_1	D_0	Description
0	0	0	one copy
0	0	1	two copies—close spacing
0	1	0	two copies—medium spacing
0	1	1	three copies—close spacing
1	0	0	two copies—wide spacing
1	0	1	one copy—double sized player
1	1	0	three copies—medium spacing
1	1	1	one copy—quad sized player

The number-size register offers an easy way to modify the appearance and behavior of player sprites. *Combat* offers the most transparent use of this technique, using the number-size settings as the basis for many of its twenty-seven game variations. The biplane and jet plane variations that double, triple, or stretch one or both sprites use the number-size register to accomplish what would otherwise have had to be done through complex on-the-fly graphics processing or by storing additional sprites in precious ROM—only 2K of which was allotted for *Combat*. For example, variation 19 is "2 vs. 2 Bi-Plane," in which each player controls two planes that fly in formation. This variation does nothing more than set both $NUSIZ_0$ and $NUSIZ_1$ to the binary value %00000001, which corresponds to "two copies—close" in the number-size register table provided earlier. Variation 20 is "1 vs. 3 Bi-Plane," in which player one controls a large plane and player two controls three small ones in formation. This variation sets $NUSIZ_0$ to %00100111 (quad-sized player) and $NUSIZ_1$ to %00000110 (three copies—close).

These number-size registers alter the timing and frequency with which the TIA adjusts the color value to draw each sprite. For example, when doubled (%00000001), the TIA draws each bit of a sprite for two color clocks instead of one.

Variation 20 demonstrates the opportunities and limitations of the number-size registers for gameplay modification. Player 1 is at a disadvantage, because that player's plane is larger and therefore more vulnerable to fire. To counterbalance, this variation increases the size of the missile so that player 1 does not have to be as accurate: the third flipped bit in %00100111 increases the size of player 1's missile to 4 TIA clock cycles, or four times the size of player 2's missiles. However, when player 2's sprites triple, the TIA automatically triples its missiles as well, making things easier again for player 2. A more appropriate orthogonal design approach for this variation might have been to speed up the larger player and/or the missile, thereby offsetting player 1's increased target footprint. However, to do so would have required changes in the game's logic, not just in the data settings that map variation to sprite appearance. The trade-offs involved in such a decision are typical of those faced in VCS game programming.

Interestingly, the game variation matrix is duplicated almost exactly as it appears in code in the *Combat* manual (figure 2.5). The grid of options in the manual is expanded beyond the compact representation it has in ROM, but the manual's table is more or less just implemented in code as a place where the program looks up the features of a particular game.

Paddles, *Video Olympics*, and AI

Video Olympics was another of the original launch titles for the Atari VCS, hitting the shelves before the Amateur Sports Act of 1978 restricted the use of the term "Olympics." The cartridge was coded by Joe Decuir, a programmer of *Combat* and a developer of the VCS chipset. Initially, Decuir wrote a version of *Video Olympics* as test code for the VCS hardware; he later developed that into the finished product.

As *Combat* was the VCS *Tank*, so *Video Olympics* was the system's *Pong*. The first set of game variations is in fact called "Pong," and the Sears version of the cartridge is *Pong Sports*. The cartridge includes fifty variations and allows the use of one or two pairs of paddles—each pair plugs into one of the VCS's two ports—to support up to four players at once. The difficulty switches can be used to adjust the size of the bats, and different variants allow special moves such as "whammy" (change the angle of deflection as the ball is hit) and "catch" (grab the ball).

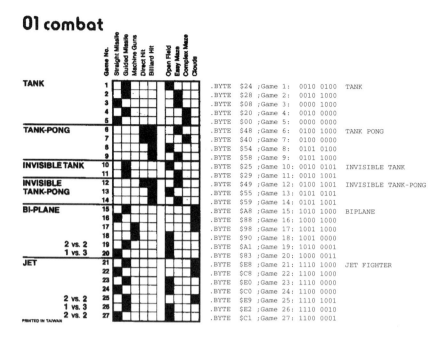

2.5 The game variation reference from the *Combat* manual next to a section of data in the game's program ROM (obtained by disassembling the cartridge's machine code). The tables differ visually because two columns have been switched. The high bit (the leftmost one) is used in the code to indicate whether the variant is a tank game or a jet game.

Four-player *Pong* was provided by certain other dedicated Atari systems from 1977, including *Ultra Pong Doubles*, which Sears labeled *Pong Sports IV*. This product offered sixteen game variations in four categories: Pong, Hockey, Street Tennis, and Street Hockey. There was also a basketball *Pong*-like game available for the home, in Atari's 1977 *Video Pinball*. But no system offered the array of choices that *Video Olympics* did: Pong, Super Pong, Pong Doubles, Quadrapong, Soccer, Foozpong, Handball, Ice Hockey, Basketball, and Volleyball. True, some of the available game variations seem to be particularly strange, unplayable caricatures of sports, but perhaps this feature of *Video Olympics* was prescient. In the years after its release, the Atari VCS would serve as a platform for a huge variety of games. Some of these would prove to be great fun, while some would be inscrutable flops.

From the standpoint of the system's launch in 1977, the really interesting game variations in *Video Olympics* may have been not the four-player ones but the two one-player "Robot Pong" variants that were offered—the first ones on the cartridge. In the austere 2K cartridge, amid the fifty variations in numerous different categories, there was this particular spark of something that would later, with reference to other simulated computer game opponents, come to be called "artificial intelligence."

Video Olympics, along with Larry Kaplan's Video Chess the following year, were early examples of AI in games on any platform—but they were not the first by any means. Way back in 1956, Edmund Berkeley created a tic-tac-toe computer called "Relay Moe."[5] Constructed of relays and using a cam to alter a display, Relay Moe could play a perfect game of tic-tac-toe, winning or drawing every time. Berkeley's effort was not the first game-playing AI; Christopher Strachey had created a checkers-playing program on the Manchester Mark I some five years earlier.[6] But Relay Moe offered something special. It could be tuned to play an imperfect game.

Relay Moe was designed for a single purpose, and its unusual design reflects choices that are suited to the game of tic-tac-toe. As a general-purpose computer and videogame system, the constraints of the Atari VCS made AI programming fairly difficult, mainly because the limited number of processor cycles available between screen draws made complex computer behavior difficult to implement. Video Chess managed to offer a complex AI opponent, though, one capable of playing a convincing game of chess. Chess is obviously much more complicated in many ways than is Pong. To deal with this complexity, Video Chess was also able to take advantage of the slow pace of a typical chess game to increase the number of processor cycles used in making a move. Chess is played asynchronously—one player moves and then waits for the other. For this reason, Kaplan was able to split up the computational work of the chess-playing AI across multiple frames of the television picture. From the player's perspective, the computer appears to be "thinking" about its move during a game of Video Chess. The AI provided on the cartridge left some people impatient, but it did work remarkably well.

A similar technique couldn't have driven the AI in the Robot Pong variants of Video Olympics. Pong may be a significantly simpler game than chess, but it also much faster-paced. Rapid screen updates and twitchy response times are hallmarks of the game, and are features also found in many other early and contemporary video games. Furthermore, Video Olympics was a 2K cartridge that already boasted fifty game variations.

Storing a large set of instructions or lookup tables wasn't an option for its Robot Pong games.

Relay Moe's capability for perfect and imperfect play offers an interesting example of an adaptable opponent—an early AI within a game. Playing against a perfect tic-tac-toe competitor, and playing well, can only ever result in a draw. This may be computationally impressive the first time, but it isn't very fun. Opponents, computer or human, become interesting when they make mistakes—or more accurately, when it becomes clear that they might make mistakes under certain circumstances. Such mistakes highlight weaknesses, which players can exploit as part of a strategy.

Edmund Berkeley realized this fact and made it possible to adjust Relay Moe to play less than perfectly. In the case of tic-tac-toe, an occasional mistake is the only way to avoid a draw against a good player. Once the player knows the machine has the capacity to make mistakes, playing multiple matches with the computer becomes much more interesting. The same is true of playing tic-tac-toe against a human player subject to distraction or to an occasional flub.

Effective game AI needs to simulate good, "intelligent" human behavior. But as Relay Moe demonstrates, convincing AI also needs to simulate certain types of *unintelligent* human behavior, in the form of mistakes that make play more fun. The AI in the Robot Pong games does this by simulating both the correct placement of the paddle and the occasional imperfection inherent to a real human opponent.

The AI moves the paddle to match the vertical position of the ball at any given time, appearing to follow it across the playfield. Such an algorithm probably does not match most human players' technique when playing *Pong*, but it is not entirely far-fetched, either. Following the puck with the paddle is a common strategy in tabletop air hockey. If the computer simply did this and matched the AI player's paddle position to that of the ball at all times, the result would be even worse than the perfect tic-tac-toe machine. The game wouldn't just be a draw—it would be one in which the human player could never score a single point. To avoid this blunder, Robot Pong's AI slows itself down, never quite following the ball exactly while still appearing to do so.

The effect is accomplished very simply. When the ball is first served, the computer positions the AI paddle so that its top edge is vertically aligned with the ball. To move the ball, the program adjusts its vertical position by an offset value each frame of up to ± 2 scan lines. This value corresponds with the direction in which the ball is moving (up or down), as well as with its speed. Each time the kernel adjusts the vertical position of the ball, it also adjusts the paddle.

To help simulate the human error inherent in precise paddle positioning, the AI paddle skips its vertical adjustment every eight frames. The resulting behavior is visibly unnoticeable, but it allows the computer player's aim to drift enough that it occasionally misses the ball. It is also technically trivial to implement, requiring only a simple mask using the binary AND operation, for which there exists a corresponding 6502 instruction. The programmer can test to see whether the result is zero with another single opcode, branching if needed to skip the instructions that move the paddle.

Even this behavior must be modified slightly for the game to work at all. If the AI player simply stopped tracking the ball every eight frames, it would be hopelessly out of sync within a few seconds. To prevent this, the AI follows a secondary ball-tracking plan near the top and bottom of the playfield. If the ball collides with one of these walls when the paddle is also aligned with it, the paddle readjusts, recovering from any drift that had accumulated since the ball last struck the wall. The result is a stochastic misalignment and realignment of computer paddle and ball.

Together, these two techniques produce a convincing robot player of *Pong*—one that makes mistakes, but not too frequently. One way for the human player to take advantage of the AI's behavior is to depress the paddle controller's single, red button; this speeds up the ball when it strikes the player's on-screen paddle. However, if the computer opponent successfully returns the ball, it will be going just as fast, making the less precise, more fallible human player more likely to miss the shot. Another technique—one that takes into account the AI behavior more directly—is to attempt to bank the ball off a wall on the human player's side of the screen. Because the AI readjusts itself only when it meets the ball at the top or bottom of the playfield, a fast-moving banked ball at a large angle has a higher chance of gliding past the computer's paddle. A slice can increase the angle of the ball, causing it to move ±3 scan lines compared to the computer paddle's ±2, and thus increasing the player's likelihood of getting a shot past the computer.

The Robot Pong games were coded to animate a computer opponent so that a human player would find playing against it challenging and fun, and they were coded about as well as any one-player Pong-like game has been. In fact, the Robot Pong variants were convincing enough to serve as the basis for a new one-player mode in the version of *Pong* that shipped in the 1999 Windows PC collection *Atari Arcade Hits: Volume 1*. As developer Jeff Vavasour explained, "The original Pong could only be played by two human players, as it had no AI. To maintain the sense of authenticity, our computer AI with the default settings plays by the exact same rules as the AI found in Atari 2600 Video Olympics."[7] It is interesting that by 1999, the very idea of a game that *required* two players (rather than serving as an optional addition to a single-player game) was unusual enough to give the creators of the *Atari Arcade Hits* collection pause. The addition of a one-player mode to the emulated coin-op *Pong* attempts to balance authenticity and marketability in the adaptation. The *Video Olympics* AI works in a fairly simple way, but it is effective enough to be fun, and was effective enough to contribute to the development of computerized opponents in late-1970s video games.

Though there were several other successful paddle games for the Atari VCS, including the arcade ports *Breakout* and *Warlords*, the potentiometer of *Pong* gave way quickly to the joystick, the controller that became emblematic of the system. Later releases of VCS-compatible systems such as the Atari 2600 Jr. and Atari Flashback 2 included only the joystick controller.

Revisiting *Combat*

At the gaming retailers' expo E3 in May 2000, Harmon Leon of the now-defunct gaming site DailyRadar.com set up a booth that featured an aluminum-foil-wrapped Atari VCS with a *Combat* cartridge plugged into it. Leon announced through his megaphone and using a hand-lettered sign that this system was actually a new game called *CyberBattle 2000*, enticing several expo attendees to play it.[8] A humorous review of *CyberBattle 2000* appeared on DailyRadar.com after the conference and read, in part:

> It's refreshing to see a videogame that pares down creativity, revealing the very essence of gameplay. The graphics engine, designed by ex-Rare and id programmers, manages to recreate the feeling of a battlefield, without overwhelming the player with unnecessary distractions. The glowing battlecraft reveal a subtle design ethic unmatched by any similar title. . . . Musical influences have been borrowed from many sources, most notably Leonard Cohen and Philip Glass. The result is an ambient simplicity with a Mooglike analog vibe. . . . [That] brings us to the plot—a plot so delicately strung that absolute attention must be paid as it unwinds delicate threads of intrigue and suspense. The twist at the end of the game is stunning. *Cyberbattle 2000* revels in the fact that no other game will ever achieve this perfect balance between simplicity and style.[9]

Today, many remember *Combat* fondly and some still play it occasionally. Although the DailyRadar.com review was mockery (mainly of videogame reviewing rather than *Combat* itself), there are plenty of sincere contemporary reviews that are quite positive. One reviewer calls the cartridge a "true classic" and notes, "While the graphics can only be described as grotesque, *Combat* has great gameplay. . . . Besides *Pong*, *Combat* may be the ultimate two-player game."[10] Another writes, "This is the Charlie Chaplin of the game world. . . . Looks crap but is really, really good."[11] Although there is some dissent, most of those who have written about *Combat* recently still praise it. It has been rereleased in recent years as part of the two-player Atari Flashback 2, a VCS-compatible unit with forty built-in games. These include a never-before-released sequel developed by Atari: *Combat 2*.

Reappearances of *Combat* itself are hardly the only legacy of the cartridge. Furthermore, it is not really reasonable to look for signs of *Combat*'s influence in specific categories such as later tank games and games that involve two-player battles. What the cartridge really contributed was a compelling demonstration of the Atari VCS, an advertisement for the system's two-player capabilities and its ability to pack many game variants into a single cartridge. *Combat* showed that the system could be enjoyed by many people, and that through difficulty settings and variants, people of different ages and aptitudes could play against each other enjoyably. In this sense, a later tank game such as *Spectre* may be a less remarkable descendant of *Combat* than is *Wii Sports*.

Combat stood first in the line of VCS cartridges, where it made a strong case to players and set a good example for developers. It certainly didn't exhaust the gameplay, graphics, or sound capabilities of the Atari VCS, but it showed off what the system was made to do and how it could be fun. Thanks to the programmers who would continue developing this line of cartridges at Atari and elsewhere, the platform would go on to support all sorts of innovation and to do things that the original VCS developers—and the programmers of *Combat*—almost certainly never imagined.

What video game could be more typical than an action-adventure? Any canon of computer games would certainly include the *Ultima* series, along with *The Legend of Zelda* and its successors; *Tomb Raider* is also an action-adventure game, and the *Grand Theft Auto* series borrows from that genre as well as others, such as the driving game.

Before all of these looms *Adventure*, Warren Robinett's second game for Atari. (His first, *Slot Racers*, was a combat racing game in which each player navigated a rudimentary slot car through a maze, attempting to fire a bazooka and hit the opposing player's car.) Robinett was the first Atari employee who had a degree in computer science, which may have had something to do with his visiting the Stanford Artificial Intelligence Laboratory and encountering another kind of maze there—one that would inspire the cartridge he created. The game he devised was not at all obvious at the time, but it would manage to establish the basic conventions of the graphical adventure.

Text Adventure into Action Adventure

A few years before Robinett rode his bike between Sunnyvale and Menlo Park, Don Woods added on to Will Crowther's code to complete the canonical version of the PDP-10 program *Adventure*. This *Adventure*, which made its appearance in 1976, was the first example of the form that would be called the "text adventure" and that later still would be called "interactive fiction." Crowther and Woods's original specimen combined some elements from the fantasy roleplaying game *Dungeons and Dragons* with aspects of the experience of caving, one of Crowther's hobbies. The canonical PDP-10 *Adventure*, like Crowther's even earlier version, has no graphics whatsoever. It divides space into discrete areas and explains those spaces using textual descriptions.

To interact with the game, the player issues textual commands to move through an often-confusing series of rooms and passages and undertake actions in those spaces. The player moves by naming compass directions (GO NORTH) or destinations (BUILDING), and performs actions by writing simple verb-noun sentences (GET LAMP). The program can be accessed on a fancy video terminal, but a Teletype or other print terminal, of the sort that was common in the mid-1970s, works just as well. A typical exchange looked like this:

>**go west**
It is now pitch dark. If you proceed you will likely fall into a pit.
>**light lamp**
Your lamp is now on.
You are in a room filled with debris washed in from the surface.
A low wide passage with cobbles becomes plugged with mud and debris here, but an awkward canyon leads upward and west. A note on the wall says "MAGIC WORD XYZZY".
A three foot black rod with a rusty star on an end lies nearby.

Robinett became enamored with the PDP-10 *Adventure*. Once *Slot Racers* was complete, he was determined to create a VCS adaptation of the textual game.[1] Reflecting on his work twenty-five years later, Robinett called this effort "a combination of passion and stubbornness."[2] His passion was for Crowther and Woods's game, and his stubbornness was a refusal to let the Atari VCS's utterly different hardware prevent him from adapting the game and paying homage to it.

Around the time when Robinett became fascinated with the PDP-10 *Adventure*, some programmers at MIT did as well. Dave Lebling and Marc Blanc, working with Tim Anderson and Bruce Daniels, kept the format of the text adventure for their *Adventure*-like game, which they called *Zork*. (This term was used at MIT to designate an incomplete program.) They developed an elaborate PDP-10 version of *Zork* by 1979, at which point three of them joined forces with others to found Infocom, a company which became the major commercial text-adventure developer in the United States. Infocom released versions of *Zork* for many home microcomputer platforms of the early 1980s, including the Apple][, the Commodore 64, the Atari 400/800, and the IBM PC.

The development of the text-adventure genre, on the one hand, and the action-adventure genre, on the other, forked off from Crowther and Woods's *Adventure* at a very early point, long before the general public even knew that *Adventure* existed. This type of inspiration and divergence, caused by developers' casual encounters with research or amateur work and their interest in reimplementing or improving it, was common at the time. The PDP-10 *Adventure* was an experiment, a diversion created by hobbyists. Although it is easy to forget about this in today's highly corporate videogame marketplace, many important games have been developed in such a way.

The influence of the text-based *Adventure* on Robinett was quite accidental. Today, the market pulls many of the strings of videogame production. But the canonical PDP-10 *Adventure* was never purchased or sold; it was, instead, distributed in what was informally called the public domain. Anyone with the right platform could install and play the PDP-10 *Adventure* if they wanted to do so. This helps to explain why Microsoft was able to publish a port of *Adventure* in 1981 without consulting or paying Crowther and Woods, and why Atari could market Robinett's more distinctive VCS version using the same title.

Virtual Space

Text adventures render their setting and their spaces as language. This may seem like an unnatural mode in which to understand something spatial, but text adventures can represent space effectively, even portraying spaces in figurative or unusual ways to create interesting puzzles for the player.

The Atari VCS was not built to present text in the way that a PDP-10 or a TRS-80 or an Apple][was. It has no images of characters built into ROM and no facilities for text rendering and manipulation. Although VCS programmers did devise ways to allow something akin to typing on the machine, these solutions were kludges at best, never offering the kind of keyboard experience that was familiar to users.

Instead, the console is engineered to display graphics and play sounds. As described in the previous chapter, the machine offers a low-resolution playfield, two sprite graphics (each with a corresponding missile), and a ball graphic. Translating the first text adventure had to mean somehow doing with the Atari VCS's primitive graphics what the PDP-10 *Adventure* did with prose. Robinett's main innovation in *Adventure* was devising an approach to the graphical representation of a player's movement through a complex space. Robinett explained: "I had a scheme for adapting the text dialogue of *Adventure* into a video game: use the joystick to move around, show one room at a time on the video screen, and show objects in the room as little shapes."[3]

Where a text adventure would have defined a single location, or "room," with a description, a graphical adventure would display an image of a virtual space on the screen. The player would move a representation of a character around in this space. And to move between portions of the larger space of which the room is a part, the player would move that representation of a character to one of the edges of the current space, so that it would appear on the opposite end of an adjacent space, which the game would draw anew. Future action-adventure games—most notably, *The Legend of Zelda*—used this same method of rendering a large virtual space in screen-sized segments.

To understand how Robinett implemented his solution in *Adventure*, it is necessary to say more about TIA playfield graphics and Robinett's own experience authoring *Slot Racers*.

To give the sense of a room or enclosed space, *Adventure* needed real graphical edges. As Robinett said, "In a text adventure game, a room is a single location. Although there are passages to other rooms, the room itself has no internal structure. . . . A single room can show a simple maze on the screen, with passages going off the screen to other (as yet unseen) maze rooms. The walls of the maze, of course, block . . . movement. A 4- or 5-room maze can be quite complicated."[4]

The problem is one of boundaries. Spaces need to have well-defined boundaries to be comprehensible. *Combat* and *Slot Racers* already made use of a facility of the Atari VCS to provide such boundaries: TIA playfield graphics, those low-resolution screen graphics that the program can specify in blocks. The display supports forty blocks of playfield per line. The program can change these between (or even during) each scan line of the television display.

To reduce the amount of memory on the TIA chip, Decuir and Miner devoted only three bytes of storage to playfield graphics, of which two and a half are actually used by the display. The registers' names are PF0, PF1, and PF2 (PF stands for "PlayField"). PF0 stores only half a byte, or four bits, and the other two store a full byte, or eight bits. Two eight-bit and one four-bit playfield storage locations amount to twenty bits of space (8 + 8 + 4 = 20), or exactly half of the forty blocks actually displayed on the screen. The TIA can be configured to automatically double or mirror those

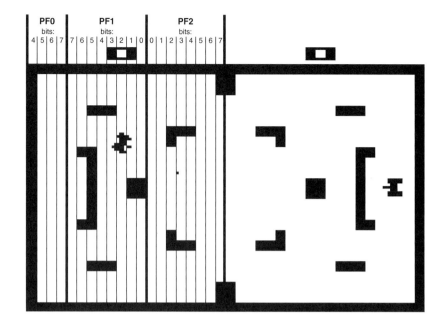

3.1 A clear view of the horizontal symmetry that is usually seen in VCS playfield graphics—in this case, from *Combat*. The left half of the screen shows how the playfield data maps to the TIA's playfield registers. The TIA does not write each of the three PF registers in the same order: PF0 is written from the low bit to the high bit of the upper nybble (half-byte), PF1 is written from the high bit to the low bit, and PF2 is written from the low bit to the high bit. This method simplified the chip's circuit design, but it also made complex playfield routines like scrolling more difficult to program.

twenty blocks on the second half of the display. The programmer does this by setting (mirror) or clearing (double) the lowest bit of the TIA's CTRLPF (ConTRoL PlayField) register.

This capability of the Atari VCS most directly accounts for the horizontal symmetry of the playing field in *Combat* and *Slot Racers* (figure 3.1). In *Combat*, the walls in the tank variants and the clouds in both sorts of plane variants are drawn with playfield graphics. The tracks in *Slot Racers* are drawn in the same way. The reason for this symmetry being implemented in hardware in the first place had to do with the two-player inspirations for the machine. *Pong* and *Tank* were two-player games, with a human controlling each player. The games set both players up with similar tools and obstacles—one paddle or tank, the same set of walls, and so forth, literally evening the playfield, as is culturally conventional for games of this sort.

Forming an arena accounts for one of two uses of playfield graphics in early games like *Combat* and *Slot Racers*. In addition, they are used at the top of the screen to display scores. One of the innovations that distinguished *Home Pong* from *Tennis* on the Odyssey was a score display of the sort that the arcade *Pong* also sported. Playfield graphics in a doubled state are used to render the score. Setting the second bit in the CTRLPF register described earlier gives the left half of the color of player 1, and the right half the color of player 2.

The TIA is responsible for taking the graphics data and color stored in each of its registers and modulating the CRT to display the result properly. For this reason, it is very easy to determine whether two different elements (such as a sprite and the playfield) overlap. Overlaps of different registers on common positions are called "collisions." The TIA provides a set of programmer-readable collision latches for each pair of graphical objects, indicating whether the two objects are intersecting. Collision detection is a common feature of graphical video games, but it is often a bit tricky to code up. Thanks to the TIA's provision for collision detection in hardware, it is easy to implement things such as shooting or being shot by missiles, running into a wall, or consuming something. All the program has to do is read from a set of memory-mapped registers reserved for collision.

Combat and *Slot Racers* had already used collision detection to prevent their tanks and cars from passing through maze barriers. The VCS *Adventure* extended this use of collision detection to define spaces to explore rather than just spaces where one can seek cover from incoming fire. Likewise, the cartridge's translation of text-adventure space into action-adventure space comes from the use of playfield graphics as enclosures. Whereas the PDP-10 *Adventure* describes the interiors of spaces, the VCS *Adventure* defines their boundaries; exploration in action-adventure games involves testing and discovering the edges of spaces at least as much as it involves exploring their interiors. To allow for this type of exploration, Robinett had to devise a new way to use playfield graphics to describe a larger space.

Movement

Both the VCS *Adventure* and its PDP-10 inspiration construct a large virtual space by coupling many smaller spaces together and allowing the player to move between them. But though text adventures emphasize movement *between* spaces, action-adventure games emphasize movement *through* and *within* spaces. In the VCS *Adventure*, the player does not merely press the joystick in a compass direction to go to the next screen. Rather, the player moves a square around on that screen, perhaps choosing to continue to the edge so that the square moves off the current screen and onto the next screen.

This movement set the standard for later action-adventure games, including the tile-based games in the *Ultima* and *The Legend of Zelda* series. Even though most contemporary action-adventure games use three-dimensional (3D) rendered worlds rather than two-dimensional (2D) top-down ones, the concept of movement from room to room, as in a castle or dungeon, persists. Robinett's solution to contiguous movement through space may seem obvious to us now, but it required a great deal of engineering, given the nature of VCS screen graphics. The *Adventure* manual's quaint explanation of screen-to-screen movement testifies to how novel and unusual the scheme was at the time: "Each area shown on your television screen will have one or more barriers or walls, through which you CANNOT pass. There are one or more openings. To move from one area to an adjacent area, move 'off' the television screen through one of the openings; the adjacent area will be shown on your television screen." More than any other feature of the machine, the register-based method of drawing the screen a line at a time as discussed in the previous chapter made some styles of play and forms of game harder than others to implement. Consider Warren Robinett's explanation of his early work on *Adventure* development: "A month later, I had a prototype: the player could move a small square "cursor" from screen to screen, picking up the little colored shapes to be found on some of the screens, which were connected edge to edge. And there was a pesky dragon that chased the cursor around, trying to eat it. Exhausted, I went on vacation."[5] Robinett actually left the intense work environment of Atari at that point for a month-long vacation.[6] What was so taxing about programming the Atari VCS? How would a person need a month to recover from this sort of work? Programming was, after all, Robinett's job, and a VCS cartridge usually took about six months to complete. What he accomplished at this early stage probably sounds rudimentary to modern-day programmers and to today's players.

But adapting the system to allow for a large virtual space was not simple at all. To move from screen to screen, the program must track the location of the "cursor" and determine whether this location has passed beyond one of the edges of the screen. Then, the program must redraw the new screen and position the cursor at the opposite end.

This operation is complex, because the VCS display is not divided into pixels as a modern raster display is. Instead, the screen is built out of units that correspond to television scan lines. To manage vertical positioning, most VCS programs store the starting horizontal location of an object in RAM. On each scan line, the program checks to see whether the drawing of a sprite should be started or continued. Determining whether an object is at the top or bottom of the screen is relatively simple. It is just a matter of comparing the object's scan line position to that of the top or bottom boundary of a counter used in drawing the visible display. Because the processor can ask the TIA to report when it is about to start a new scan line, precise vertical positioning is straightforward.

Precise horizontal position is another matter. There is no simple way for the programmer to "poll" the TIA for its current horizontal position; the television display doesn't decompose into logical horizontally divided units as simply as it does into vertically divided scan lines. For this reason, accomplishing horizontal movement on the VCS requires a different technique.

As detailed in the previous chapter, the unit that most resembles a pixel on the horizontal axis of a VCS image is called a "color clock." To move objects horizontally, the TIA provides a register for each that allows the programmer to move it *relative* to its last position, left by up to eight color clocks or right by up to seven. To execute such a move, the programmer strobes a register called HMOVE at the start of a scan line.

The TIA's eight-bit registers do not overflow; adding 1 to 255 yields 0, adding 2 to 255 yields 1, and so on. (The machine is incapable of throwing an error.) This means that the hardware is set up for horizontal wraparound, of the sort seen in *Asteroids*, a game that also wraps the playing field vertically. If an object moves to the right edge of the screen, the piece of it that goes off the screen will "naturally" begin to appear on the other side. (This is exactly what happens to planes and their missiles in the *Combat* plane games; the only thing preventing the same sort of wraparound in the tank games is the solid, rectangular boundary of the playfield.) Unless the program keeps track of an object's position in RAM, it has no simple way to tell where on the screen the object currently appears. To move the *Adventure* player from screen to screen, then, Robinett used an additional routine to keep track of horizontal movement so that it was possible to respond to player movement off the left or right of the screen.

Robinett's initial month of prototype development included more than just player movement and room changes, but the relative difficulty of simply determining the horizontal position of the player and deciding whether a new room had to be drawn reveals a great deal about the VCS *Adventure*'s technical innovation. In *Combat*, an adaptation and expansion of *Tank* had been developed jointly with the system and had helped guide the hardware design of the Atari VCS in the first place. *Adventure* required the creative adaptation of the machine's technical features for new, unforeseen purposes. Such innovation, while certainly possible, was not always easy. The VCS *Adventure* provides an example of a design vision that exceeded the obvious features of the VCS hardware, yet was nevertheless eventually realized.

I Am a Ball

In many contemporary games, from *World of Warcraft* to *The Godfather* to *Tony Hawk Pro Skater*, players have the option of selecting or customizing the character to use during play. Since the release of *Ultima IV* in 1985, game developers and players have called this on-screen persona an "avatar," a term borrowed from the Sanskrit word for incarnation. Avatars represent not only the fixed characters of games like *Zelda*'s Link or *Half-Life*'s Gordon Freeman, but also the more or less configurable characters of games like *World of Warcraft*.

The role of the avatar is a dual one. On one hand, this game element focuses the player on an aspect of the game's fictional world, whether this is *World of Warcraft*'s magical fantasy or *Tony Hawk*'s professional skateboarding. On the other hand, it allows the player to interpret the character based on attributes such as appearance, motivations, and values.

Avatars have a history that precedes video games. In tabletop role-playing games like *Dungeons and Dragons* (*D&D*) and even common board games like *Monopoly*, players create characters or use tokens that embody them during gameplay. One way of thinking about videogame avatars is as computational adaptations of *D&D* characters.

The PDP-10 *Adventure* was inspired by *D&D*, but also by Crowther's caving expeditions in the Kentucky mountains. In this text-based *Adventure*, the player moved around and performed actions by typing commands at a prompt. The PDP-10 *Adventure* narrates actions and environments to the player in the second person, as a *D&D* dungeon master might have done, saying things such as, "You are in a maze of twisty little passages, all alike." The combination of textual display and second-person narration reinforces the user's dual role, as a game-player solving puzzles and as a character in that game, affecting and being affected by its fictional world.[7]

In earlier video games, players also took control of an on-screen representation: the ship in *Spacewar*, the paddle in *Pong*, the tank in *Tank*. But all of these games offer predetermined actions for the player. The

Spacewar player cannot choose to leave his dogfight and go explore a neighboring galaxy. In the VCS *Adventure*, the player's personal goals couple with the game's rules and fiction through the graphical avatar.

The Atari VCS provides memory-mapped registers for two player sprites. Each one is eight bits wide. The VCS display is not high-resolution by any measure, but sprite graphics can be displayed at the highest resolution that the machine allows. Robinett chose to use the sprites to represent objects and enemies in the game: a key, a chalice, a sword, a dragon. But doing so left no player sprite available to represent the object that is actually controlled by the person playing the game.

Robinett decided to use the TIA's ball graphic for this purpose. Recall that the TIA offers registers for five movable objects—two sprites, two missiles, and one ball. The Atari VCS was engineered with *Pong* and *Tank* in mind, and so the TIA's various object registers are directly named for the objects that are used in these games. For example, the programmer turns missile and ball graphics on and off by setting or clearing the second bit of registers, ENAM0 (ENAble Missile 0), ENAM1 (ENAble Missile 1), ENABL (ENAble BaLl). Even though these names are nothing more than mnemonic labels—shortcuts that save the programmer the trouble of remembering the hexadecimal addresses of the registers—they are written into the *Stella Programmer's Guide* as the official nomenclature. All known VCS assembler programs use these names for code sections that output graphics.

There is nothing in the *Adventure* cartridge or the supporting materials to name the player's character or object. The manual also never calls the object by a distinctive name such as "avatar." It simply instructs the player in the imperative to "move." Originally, Robinett called this object "the man," but later he referred to the figure as a "cursor," since "its function, as a position indicator, is similar to the rectangular blinking cursor found on word processing screens."[8] A "position indicator" is perhaps an appropriate way to understand the avatar. It represents neither the player nor a character in the game, but the coupling between the two.

Adventure is one of the first examples of a VCS game in which the system's graphics facilities are reinvented. Robinett finds a new use not only for the ball, but also for the missile graphics, which draw the thin walls that appear in some rooms. As used in *Adventure*, the ball at least looks somewhat like a ball, although it is rectangular, as is standard on the system due to the width created by TIA color clocks. The missiles don't resemble projectiles in any way; they just look like barriers that extend across the entire height of some screens. Like all VCS graphics, missiles can be turned on or off on each scan line (by setting or clearing ENAM0/1).

Turning a missile on for the entire screen creates the thin wall we see in *Adventure*. It also prevents the programmer from having to change those registers during an entire screen draw, saving precious processing time between scan lines.

The repurposing of graphics registers has both technical and expressive consequences. Technical innovations are often understood as the creation of new technology—new materials, new chip designs, new algorithms. But technical innovation can also mean using existing technical constraints in new ways, something that produces interesting results when combined with creative goals. Designing the TIA's graphics registers to support games like *Pong* and *Tank* represents an interesting aspect of how platform development happens; reusing those graphics registers for player avatars and castle walls demonstrates a negotiation between the platform and the author's vision of a game.

Handling Items

Using a ball sprite for the player frees up the two sprite registers for other things, including enemies and objects. With regard to the items that littered the landscape, *Adventure* introduced a new convention for acquiring and using objects, one that was specific to the graphical setting and that remains in use even in today's 3D virtual spaces.

In text adventures, each action is the result of one or more verbal instructions, which the player types in at the prompt: TAKE KEY, DROP KEY. Typed input isn't an option on the Atari VCS, of course, and the system's joysticks each have only a single button. Robinett chose to use a collision between the cursor and an item to indicate that the item should be picked up. The VCS hardware collision detection provides a simple way to implement pick-up. This choice also frees the button to be used for something else—namely, dropping things. To use an item, the player just causes the held item to intersect with the target item. For example, a key collides with a portcullis to open it, a sword with a dragon to kill it.

Adapting player-object collision to correspond with TAKE, using the button to mean DROP, and having item-item collision stand in for a few other verbs depending on context (KILL, OPEN) effectively avoids the relatively large linguistic demands of text adventures and recasts them as simpler graphical demands. This shift of convention makes Robinett's *Adventure* much easier to play than the PDP-10 *Adventure*: fewer commands need to be remembered, and players can quickly learn how to operate the game. But this also compresses the possibilities of the game's fictional world. In the textual *Adventure*, the player must engage in an unusual bit of textual banter to kill the dragon: After typing "KILL DRAGON," the clarifying question "With your bare hands?" has to be answered "YES." In the VCS *Adventure*, you can kill the dragon, but not with your with bare hands, and not after a repartee like this.

There were some special touches in the VCS cartridge that were appropriate to a graphical game. Although most games of the time (and even many of today) register a death or other consequence when the player initially touches an enemy, *Adventure*'s dragon chases the player when the latter touches it. Two small touches within a specific amount of time are required to kill the avatar. Such subtle interaction between cursor and dragon notwithstanding, text adventures often focus on riddle and puzzle solving, such as navigating a maze or figuring out the purpose of an item. This practice does not carry through in action-adventure games. Instead, rapid movement through space becomes the primary mode of play, a characteristic of the genre that could also be seen in Robinett's previous game, *Slot Racers*.

Adventure's sword offers an example of the curiosity of TIA collision detection. The sword appears on the screen as a left-facing arrow. Even though the TIA does provide a register to flip sprites automatically on their horizontal axis, the sword always faces the same way, no matter how the player moves. Moreover, the sword itself looks more like an arrow; at best, it looks like a sword being held from the tip rather than the hilt. Though VCS graphics could be rightly described as "blocky," Robinett actually had far greater resolution to work with than he ended up using for the sword sprite. One reason for this decision might relate to the way collision detection functions on the machine.

In today's games, collision detection is handled in software. A computationally cheap way to accomplish this is with *bounding boxes*. In this method, boxes around each object are determined and each pair is checked for intersections. This simple and quick method is nevertheless inaccurate, because an object that does not fill its bounding box may register as colliding with something when it actually does not.

The VCS hardware collision is performed by the TIA, which checks for overlapping logic states on its multiple graphics registers. For this reason, only those bits that are turned on in the graphics registers of a sprite can register collision. In other words, the parts of a sprite that are actually seen are the only ones subject to colliding. Thanks to a relatively simple circuit on the TIA, the Atari VCS offers more precise collision detection than is done using the standard technique in modern software toolkits such as Adobe Flash (see figure 3.2).

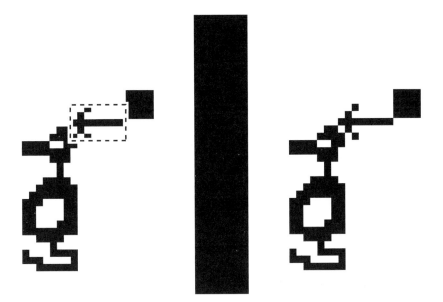

3.2 If *Adventure* had used bounding box collision detection, as on the left, this arrangement of sword and dragon would indicate a collision, because the box enclosing the former intersects the latter. Because the VCS hardware implements collision detection by overlapping bits, as on the right, there is actually no collision in this situation.

There can be a downside to precise collision detection. Unless an item's image strikes precisely against its target, no collision will register, even in cases in which one would be desirable. The arrow-like end of the sword expands the collision surface of the weapon and also helps the player orient an attack in that direction.

The shapes of objects were not the only thing motivated by technical intricacies. One object was specifically added to work around a problem in the system for dropping and picking up object. As Robinett explained, "The magnet was created because of a bug. Sometimes the key to a castle would get dropped inside a wall and be unable to be picked up, so the magnet, which attracted other objects, was a solution to that problem."[9]

Getting Lost

Text adventures are characterized by discrete spaces with detailed textual explanations to help players remember, understand, and navigate the world that the game presents. Because the text adventure describes spaces using only text, when those spaces become complex or obfuscated, as in the case of Crowther and Woods's classic mazes, the player is often driven to somehow map the space (usually on paper, using an graph-like map or an adjacency grid), so it can be understood and navigated. Very clever or very spatially oriented players might be able to do this in their heads, but more often, players would attempt to draw a map. The early player of Crowther and Woods's *Adventure* would likely be sitting at a print terminal, in which case paper would be easily available; a pencil (used to correct programs) might also be already at hand. Drawing maps on paper, as people did in some pre-*Adventure* games such as *Hunt the Wumpus*, became an important part of the process of solving spatial puzzles in early text adventures.

The VCS *Adventure* could not rely on the availability of paper and the willingness of players to use it to map locations, but it could manage to avoid the complexities and confusions involved in the textual representation of space in the first place. As Robinett explained his perspective: "A maze is a geometric construction in space; the positioning of its walls defines a maze. Video graphics do an excellent job of capturing the geometry of a maze. By contrast, using sentences to describe a maze is inefficient and piecemeal."[10]

This solution does not demand as much work from the player. Instead of requiring paper and pencil, the game maintains coherence between all visited spaces by keeping exits and entrances consistent. A player can manage to remember that the avatar came from the left and is moving to the right.

The obfuscation of space is still a characteristic design element in the VCS *Adventure*. The game's labyrinths typically cross multiple screens, with branches near the edges of the screen. This design makes it harder for the player to mentally map the maze in its entirety, creating the feeling of being lost. Additionally, a maze of multiple screens allows for the symmetrical playfields on a single screen to create asymmetrical mazes when stitched together. *Adventure* also includes wormholes that move the player into separate sections of its spaces—spaces that don't reconnect with themselves in expected ways. At the start of the game, going down, left, and up puts the player at the mouth of the blue labyrinth. But moving right from there—which should put the player back into a room he passed through on the way—exposes another part of the blue labyrinth! Worse, the blue labyrinth also wraps around itself, transporting the player from one side to the other as if by magic. This use of inconsistent maze geometry (see figure 3.3) further confuses the player's sense of location.[11] The same effect can be found in the mazes

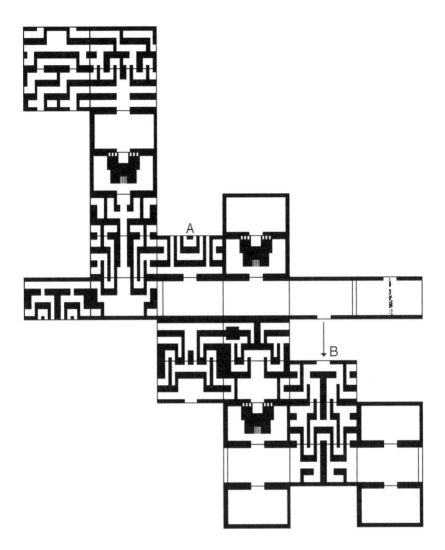

3.3   This map of the world in *Adventure* makes the game's spatial inconsistencies clear. The screen below the point marked A seems to have only dead ends on the right side, but there are actually exits there that wrap around to the opposite side of the screen to the left. Likewise, moving to the screen below point B requires a jump across a place where the map does not exist. (This image is based on a map by Maurice Molyneaux. For an annotated version, see http://www.atarihq.com/2678/adv-map1.gif.)

in the PDP-10 *Adventure*, although those are portrayed using word rather than image.

Confusing spaces have frequently been seen in action-adventure games. *The Legend of Zelda* took *Adventure*'s four-directional maze pattern and added a set of movements through the same maze as a symbol for finding its exit. These "lost woods," as they are called in the first version of that game, trap the player completely until the proper sequence of directions (up, left, down, left) is discovered, allowing escape. The traversal of space has become a standard way to require the discovery of a particular input sequence, something that had been previously done through the subtlety of language.

Another method of spatial confusion introduced in *Adventure* is occlusion. In early text adventures, rooms and caverns are often dark and their contents and exits are not visible. The player was typically able to use a lamp or some other light source to illuminate these areas, whose contents would then be described with text.

In a text adventure, illumination is usually all or nothing: a room is either lit or dark. But this design doesn't work for a graphical game like the VCS *Adventure*. A dark room would just be a black screen. The text adventure always provides a facility for direct input—the text prompt—but there would be no obvious graphical analogue in a totally dark room in the VCS *Adventure*.

Robinett managed to implement occlusion using a different method, one that would come to be called "the fog of war" in later adventure and strategy games. "Fog of war" is a military term that refers to the ambiguity and confusion experienced in the theater of war. In games, it usually refers to a lack of visual information on a map. Areas that have been explored or settled become visible, whereas those that have not remain shrouded or entirely black. Board games like *Stratego* implement a kind of fog of war by hiding the identity of opposing units. Tabletop miniature games often track the location of units like tanks on a separate record or even a separate board.

Variations 2 and 3 of *Adventure* introduce catacombs, which take the form of an orange labyrinth. These catacombs are darkened, and the player can only see the maze's walls within a small distance around him. To accomplish the occlusion, Robinett simply made the floor and walls the same color. The walls in *Adventure* are drawn, after all, using playfield graphics. The color for the playfield and the background are set by writing the same eight-bit color value to each of two registers, COLUPF and COLUBK. The ball always takes on the color of the playfield, which explains why the cursor matches the walls and why its color changes from screen to screen.

To create the "light" that emanates from the player, *Adventure* uses a widened square sprite that is orange. The player is centered inside this "box," and both are moved together. The same TIA register that controls playfield reflection or mirroring can also be set to draw the playfield either underneath the sprite (the default setting) or on top of it (as in *Combat*'s plane variants). In the catacombs, the playfield is set to draw on top of the sprite, making the area around the player cursor appear to glow with light. The effect is sophisticated, but it is implemented in a straightforward way. The circle of light is just another carried object, no different from a sword or a key. A similar implementation of partial darkness—although one that is more advanced—can be seen in Atari's 1982 VCS game *Haunted House.*

Some video games implement the fog of war as a way to hide knowledge that the player can discover. In *Civilization*, once a player has explored a part of the world's terrain, that square always remains visible, as if the society had entered it into an almanac. Other games implement the fog of war as transitory knowledge. In *Warcraft*, a player must have units in a region to be able to see its immediate surroundings. Both of these methods have their origins in *Adventure*'s implementation of the fog of war.

The Easter Egg

An *Easter egg* is a message, trick, or unusual behavior hidden inside a computer program by its creator. Easter eggs can be traced back at least to the early 1970s, when the TOPS-10 operating system on the PDP-10 was programmed to respond to the command "make love" with "not war?"[12] More recent Easter eggs are much more sophisticated. One recent version of *Microsoft Excel* contains a hidden flight simulator game, as does *Google Earth*.

Adventure contained the first Easter egg known to appear in any video game. The hidden message itself is reasonably simple. Warren Robinett signed his game "Created by Warren Robinett" using letters running vertically down the center of the screen (see figure 3.4). Accessing the Easter egg is less simple. To find it, the player must cross a sealed wall in the black castle using the bridge and then pick up a single black "dot" (actually a sprite graphic), which must be brought to another wall in the yellow castle. The dot grants the avatar entry into the secret room.

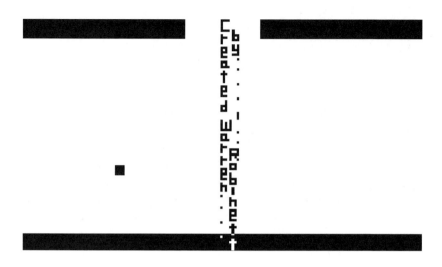

3.4 After a laborious process, the player is rewarded by being able to enter a hidden room and read this unauthorized message left by Robinett.

Robinett's motivations for signing the game have much in common with those of other Easter egg creators. Computer software, produced in business contexts or otherwise, is often impersonal. Easter eggs lay a human touch on such artifacts, reconnecting them with their creators and the craft practice of authorship. *Adventure*'s Easter egg continues this tradition.

But the state of Atari in the late 1970s offered a different context for Robinett's Easter egg. Management did not know about this element of the game and so, of course, did not approve. Robinett explained in an interview: "Each 2600 game was designed entirely by one person. But on the package it said basically 'Adventure, by Atari.' And we were only getting salaries, no cut of the huge profits. It was a signature, like at the bottom of a painting. But to make it happen, I had to hide my signature in the code, in a really obscure place, and not tell anybody. Keeping a secret like that is not easy."[13]

Robinett expressed in this statement the same sort of gripe that would cause David Crane, Larry Kaplan, Alan Miller, and Bob Whitehead to quit Atari in 1979 to start the industry's first third-party developer, Activision. Robinett and his colleagues worked long, solitary hours without much guidance or supervision—and with no royalties—and Atari then made a fortune on their games without giving them credit, publicly or internally.

Today, there are perhaps a handful of game designers whose names are well known. Will Wright, Shigeru Miyamoto, Hideo Kojima, and Richard Garriott are among them. Far fewer are directly marketed as creators of their games—Sid Meier and American McGee are the only two whose names actually precede titles of their games, in the way that an A-list film director or a best-selling author might get top billing above a work's title. Readers familiar with the labor controversies of the contemporary games industry may imagine that Robinett and others merely wanted credit or royalties. But the role of a games programmer in these years was far broader than that title suggests.

Once hired, Atari programmers were sent off to make games and were essentially told "come back when you're done."[14] Robinett's own stories of going on vacation for a month fly in the face of anything resembling micromanagement. The game programmer's job at that time was much more like a combination of what we now call the executive producer, the designer, the programmer, the artist, and the sound designer. Robinett explained:

> I believe that Atari in the early days succeeded because the games were labors of love by the programmers who worked on them. At least that was the case with my games for me. In those old far-off days, each game for the 2600 was done entirely by one person, the programmer, who conceived the game concept, wrote the program, did the graphics—drawn first on graph paper and converted by hand to hexadecimal—and did the sounds.[15]

Programmers were responsible in the early days of the Atari VCS for every aspect of the game's production up to the point where it went on the cartridge, with packaging, marketing, and sales being taken care of by others.[16] Activision later acknowledged the programmer's role by printing the creator's name on the box and cartridge of each game, as discussed in chapter 6.

Unlike some pure action games along the lines of *Combat*, adventure games offer good places to hide things, thanks to all the convoluted spaces and the techniques discussed previously. *Adventure*'s Easter egg is more than just a gimmick; it follows in the adventure game tradition by revealing a secret—the secret of the game's own production.

Atari discovered the Easter egg when a fifteen-year-old player wrote the company a letter about it. But the company never removed it from the game. Robinett has remarked that this was, at least in part, because of the cost of making a new ROM mask—roughly $10,000 in the early 1980s.[17]

Robinett designed *Adventure* specifically to overcome the machine's lack of textual input. Oddly, by the time he finally finished the game, he had also completed another title with a text-based display: *BASIC Programming*. In 1978, Atari introduced a keyboard peripheral. Despite its name, the device was really just a small rectangle of molded plastic with a grid of twelve small buttons. Plastic overlays of the type that were later used in the Mattel Intellivision helped the user understand the otherwise impenetrable combinations of keypresses needed to output simple characters. Text entry was not a simple matter of typing, but had a complexity more like that of using a chording keyboard or of inputting text on a mobile phone.

To simulate the alphanumeric display native to a standard microcomputer, Robinett used a twelve-character-per-line alphanumeric display routine that VCS virtuoso David Crane had written.[18] Though primitive compared to the Apple][, the cartridge made it possible to write and run simple programs in BASIC by typing in textual commands, much as players type short commands when playing a text adventure game.

Two decades later, amateur developers returned to this display to create text adventures of the traditional PDP-10 *Adventure* style. Greg Troutman's 1998 title *Dark Mage* lets the player direct a banished jester. Adam Thornton's 2002 version of *Lord of the Rings: The Fellowship of the Ring* repurposes the *Dark Mage* code to offer a terse text-adventure version of the first volume of Tolkien's famous epic.

Given that the VCS *BASIC Programming* was developed alongside the VCS *Adventure*, and that the text adventure did not enter mass-market public consciousness until the 1980s—after Adventure International's cassette games gained ground and Infocom released *Zork* commercially—it would not really be proper to call the action-adventure genre either an evolution or a simple descendent of the text adventure. Although Robinett's game did have its origins in the original *Adventure*, it was not influenced by a substantial tradition of text-based adventures.

The turn away from text and toward graphics started by the VCS *Adventure* was partly encouraged by games licensed from films, which began to emerge in numbers in the early 1980s, just as *Adventure* was released. During the development of the game, Atari even asked Robinett to shelve it and use the design to create a game based on the Superman license, which Warner owned. Robinett managed to foist that job off on John Dunn, sharing his code to facilitate the other game's development. *Superman* uses the same room-to-room movement of *Adventure* but employs a different perspective to let the player look across an urban landscape rather than down on an abstract dungeon. *Superman* has many of the incongruous spatial features that are also seen in *Adventure*. Flying up past the skyscrapers and onto the ground of another screen might suggest movement across a city rather than over it, but the game was more confusing than effective. *Superman* also expunged the movie's social and emotional relationships—and those of the comic books—choosing action sequences instead. Games licensed from movies have continued to follow this early VCS game in this regard.

The graphical turn in video games has been a bittersweet one. The Crowther and Woods *Adventure*, *Zork*, and the interactive fiction games that they fostered enjoyed enormous success during the 1980s, but that form was no longer marketable by the beginning of the 1990s. Interactive fiction continues to thrive among communities of writers and players without being the mass-market phenomenon it once was.[19] And despite tremendous advances in the visual fidelity of game hardware and software, the interactive engagement of contemporary adventure games has changed little since the VCS *Adventure* set the stage for the genre. Games have moved to 3D and programmers have become more concerned with polygons than pixels, but movement and collision detection remain the primary building blocks of adventure games, and, indeed, of most video games.

The arcade-inspired *Combat* was not difficult to fit onto the Atari VCS. It was one of the games developed alongside the console's hardware, influencing the latter's design. *Adventure* was inspired by *Colossal Cave Adventure*, but Robinett thoroughly reimagined the text game for the VCS platform, creating something with very different appearance and different gameplay. When Atari acquired the home console rights to Namco's hit arcade game *Pac-Man*, the company faced a different problem: that of porting the massively popular and recognizable game from a platform with totally different technical affordances.

Chasing the Blinking Coin-Ops

In the late 1970s, space shooters like *Asteroids*, *Space Invaders*, and *Galaxian* reigned in the arcades. Sports-themed games like *Pong*, war games like *Tank* and *Battlezone*, and driving games like *Night Driver* filled out the typical tavern and arcade fare. Toru Iwatani, a Japanese designer, wanted to create a different game, one that would appeal to a broader set of players. Classic *Pac-Man* lore holds that Iwatani was pondering this design problem as he was eating a pizza. Looking at the pie with one slice removed, he saw a head with its mouth agape and imagined it as an anthropomorphized character who would eat things.[1] Iwatani devised the maze as a way to structure the eating, and gave the game the title *Pakku-Man*, derived from the Japanese onomatopoeia "paku-paku"—the sound of an opening and closing mouth during eating.

Pac-Man did fairly well in Japan, but the game enjoyed wild success in the United States. *Pac-Man* was more than a video game; it was a cultural sensation, featured on the cover of *Time* and spawning dozens of licensed products including clothing, trading cards, cereal, board games, a record (*Pac-Man Fever*), television shows, and consumer goods. There are many reasons for the game's success. Novelty was undoubtedly a part of it. Journalist Chris Green has argued that *Pac-Man* filled a space in popular culture between the second and third *Star Wars* films, making it a cornerstone in 1980s popular culture. But beyond these feats of novelty and timing, *Pac-Man* was, and perhaps still is, a game that everyone will be happy to play. The game's colorful, friendly characters made everyone want to try it—boys and girls, men and women alike. Green explained:

> *Pac-Man* feels like a cartoon, from the bouncy theme music to the animated eyes on the ghosts to the forlorn sound effect as Pac-Man is apprehended and shrinks away to nothingness. Far more so than any other game before it (and many that came after), *Pac-Man* possessed elements of drama, giving names to its avatars and featuring them in brief comic interludes that played out after the player had achieved a certain level of success.[2]

It was into this cultural context that Atari released its VCS version of *Pac-Man* in 1982. The home videogame market operated alongside the arcade videogame marketplace, both enjoying significant popular and financial success. Arcade games continued to be built on ever more sophisticated technical infrastructures—ones that were increasingly distant from the Atari VCS, whose design was now more than half a decade old. Still, the massive popularity of arcade games motivated ports of these increasingly sophisticated popular coin-op games. After the VCS port of *Space Invaders* enjoyed considerable success, partly rescuing Atari from the losses of 1977–1978, the company became even more interested in arcade ports. *Pac-Man* seemed like a fruit ripe for the plucking, or perhaps even the key to Atari's continued success.

From a very high level, at a glance, a VCS *Pac-Man* conversion might seem like it would be straightforward. Although *Adventure* was a huge risk—a game totally different in form from those that preceded it—the PDP-10 *Adventure* was also entirely unknown to a popular audience, so VCS consumers had no basis for comparison. *Pac-Man* involved adapting an extremely prominent arcade title whose gameplay, graphics, sounds, and even iconography and packaging were universally understood and already based on graphical display and collisions. The reality of the project was quite challenging. The game was programmed by Tod Frye in an irrationally short time: six weeks. Worse, the game was to be manufactured as a 4K ROM rather than using the 8K bank-switched ROM that had become possible by this time. This approach was taken to save money on what would become an irresponsibly large production run of more than ten million cartridges.

Adaptation is a long-standing concern in cultural forms of all kinds. In 1972, the year of *Pong*, the film adaptation of the Mario Puzo book *The Godfather* won the Academy Award for Best Picture. In 1980, the year *Pac-Man* ruled the arcade, the Oscar went to another film developed from a book, Robert Redford's adaptation of Judith Guest's 1976 novel *Ordinary People*. Adapting novels to films is not always simple, but both media forms are good at telling stories with strong, deep, subtle characterization. Adapting films to video games poses a different set of challenges, as is discussed in chapter 7.

Pac-Man, of course, was already a video game before it was a VCS cartridge. Porting a graphical video game from one computer platform (the arcade board) to another (the Atari VCS) does not demand a change in fundamental representational or functional mode. Both versions are games, rule-based representations of an abstract challenge of hunter and hunted. Where the two versions diverge is in their technical foundations—in their platforms. And in the case of this title, those differences were significant enough to doom the VCS rendition of *Pac-Man*, by some accounts even causing a major crash in the videogame market during 1983.

Bitmaps and Mazes

The *Pac-Man* coin-op cabinet ran on a custom-made arcade system board. (Later, *Rally X* and *Ms. Pac-Man* used the same board.) It featured a Zilog Z80 CPU, a cheap eight-bit microprocessor that, along with the 6502, dominated the microcontroller market of the 1970s and 1980s.[3] At this time, arcade hardware was still much more advanced than home console hardware, because the latter needed to be so much cheaper to make home machines affordable. The Z80 CPU runs three times as fast as the 6502, but more significant differences are seen in the amounts of RAM and ROM. *Pac-Man*'s boards hold 16K of ROM, 2K of video RAM, and 2K of general RAM. The VCS *Pac-Man* cartridge is has only 4K, a quarter of the ROM in *Pac-Man*'s arcade incarnation. The 2K of RAM on the coin-op's board is sixteen times the amount in the Atari VCS. The home system, of course, has no video memory.

More important than the sheer amount of memory afforded by the arcade cabinet is how it was allocated and organized. *Pac-Man*'s video display supports a resolution of 224 × 228 pixels, split up into a 28 × 36 grid of "characters" of 8 × 8 pixels each. In *Pac-Man*'s case, a character is not a letter or number, but a bitmap tile. The 2K of video RAM is logically spit into two 1K segments, with one kilobyte used for character definitions and one for character colors. 1K is not enough storage to hold 224 eight-pixel-square bitmaps, and the same number of palette colors would need to be stored somewhere, too. The coin-op is set up so that this space is used to store references to bitmap and color data. The program draws the video display by taking the character and color references in VRAM and looking up a corresponding bitmap or color defined in *another* 4K ROM chip soldered to the board. It is this 4K ROM that holds graphical data such as the maze parts, letters, and numeric digits.

Even before we get to the game's hero and villains, *Pac-Man*'s method of drawing the maze demonstrates one of the major challenges in porting the game to the Atari VCS: time. In the arcade game, the programmer would load character values into video RAM once per maze, using the character tiles to create its boundaries. On the VCS, the maze is constructed from playfield graphics, each line of which has to be loaded from ROM and drawn separately for each scan line of the television display.

To be sure, mazes had already been displayed and explored in VCS games like *Combat*, *Slot Racers*, and *Adventure*. But these games had to construct their mazes from whole cloth, building them out of symmetrical playfields. The arcade incarnation of *Pac-Mac* demonstrates how the notion of the maze became more tightly coupled to the hardware affordances of tile-based video systems. In the arcade game, each thin wall, dot, or energizer is created by a single character from video memory. Though the method is somewhat arcane, the coin-op *Pac-Man* also allowed up to four colors per character in an eight-bit color space. (Each character defined six high bits as a "base" color—which is actually a reference to a color map of 256 unique colors stored in ROM—with two low bits added for each pixel of the bitmap.) This method allows the hollow, round-edged shapes that characterize the *Pac-Man* maze—a type of bitmap detail unavailable via VCS playfield graphics. The maze of the VCS game is simplified in structure as well as in appearance, consisting of rectangular paths and longer straight-line corridors and lacking the more intricate pathways of the arcade game (figure 4.1).

The arcade *Pac-Man*'s hardware also makes keeping track of the state of the maze relatively simple. Each pellet has a unique location on the tile grid. When a pellet is eaten, the program clears the corresponding char-

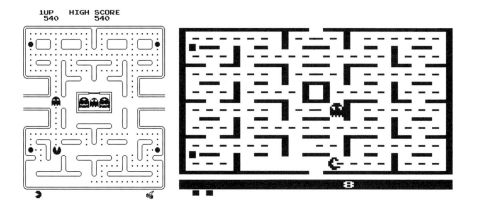

4.1 In the arcade *Pac-Man*, shown on the left, the screen is constructed of fairly high-resolution "characters," which are commonly called "tiles." What was possible on the Atari VCS using playfield graphics, as seen on the right, is not as impressive.

acter in memory, resulting in a plain black background. Tracking and displaying the current state of the pellets on the VCS is much more challenging. The pellets of the VCS *Pac-Man* are far fewer than the dots in an arcade *Pac-Man* maze, and are drawn using the same playfield graphics that define the maze borders. Because playfield graphics are used, the pellets are the same color as the walls, and are thin rectangles instead of dots—each pellet is composed of the smallest block of playfield available. The manual that comes with the VCS game tries to apologize for this divergence from the arcade version by renaming the pellets "video wafers."

The playfield, as previously noted, is formed using 20 bits of data, which are either doubled or mirrored, depending on the way the CTRLPF register is set. The original *Pac-Man* maze is horizontally symmetrical, which is very convenient. The pellets, however, disappear as the player eats them, and it is obviously impossible for *Pac-Man* to eat pellets symmetrically.

To address this challenge, Frye employed a technique for drawing asymmetric playfields. To do this, the program must first set the playfield register graphics for the left half of the screen during horizontal blank. Then, as the electron beam passes across the screen, it must change those registers just before the second half of the screen starts. This technique requires careful processor timing as well as additional RAM storage for the state of each pellet. Worse yet, the positions for each remaining pellet need to be translated from data in RAM into the unique display requirements of the TIA playfield, which does not simply write its two and a half bytes in consecutive, high-to-low bit order. To get the dots on the screen, the program tracks their states separately from their positions on-screen, performing a series of computationally expensive bitwise operations to install the pellet data into the maze playfield locations, which in turn use up valuable RAM. Maze and pellet logic—relatively simple for the arcade cabinet, given its hardware affordances—were very challenging on the Atari VCS.

Sprites

In computer graphics, a *sprite* is a 2D image composited onto a 2D or 3D scene. The Atari VCS was designed to support two sprites, each a single byte in size, set via two memory-mapped registers (named GRP0 and GRP1) on the TIA. This design clearly shows the influence of *Pong* and *Tank*—games that feature two opponents, each controlled by a human player.

The coin-op *Pac-Man* also uses sprites, but once again, its platform design offers considerably greater flexibility than does the Atari VCS. *Pac-Man* has five moving objects on the screen at once: four monsters and Pac-Man himself. The Atari VCS provides graphics registers for two movable sprites, enough for two tanks (*Combat*) or a key and a dragon (*Adventure*). But the *Pac-Man* arcade cabinet hardware supports eight different moving sprites, each a bitmap of 16 × 16 pixels. Each of these shares the same graphical properties as tile "characters," but they can also be moved to a specific (x, y) coordinate on-screen. Bitmap data for up to sixty-four sprite graphics is stored separately, in yet another 4K ROM, like the one used for characters. This style of sprite—a movable bitmap— later became the standard for home console hardware and was used in many systems, including the Intellivision and the NES.[4]

The nature of VCS sprites is very different. When the programmer stores a value in the GRP0 or GRP1 register, the TIA displays that eight-bit pattern on-screen. A VCS sprite is thus always eight bits wide, although the TIA provided a few ways of modifying the appearance of sprites on-screen.

Though a sprite is a 2D image, it is drawn (like everything on the Atari VCS) one line at a time. Each sprite register can contain only the one byte of data that it needs for drawing a single scan line. To draw, for instance, a *Space Invaders* sprite, the program has to load the byte of graphics for the alien invader that corresponds to the current line on the television display and store that value in the proper sprite graphics register during the horizontal blank, in between the drawing of two lines. To position a sprite vertically, the program has to keep track of which lines of the display have sprites on them, and to compare the current line to that value in memory before drawing. The sprite is laid out in memory like so:

Bit	7 6 5 4 3 2 1 0	Sprite:
Line 0	0 0 1 1 1 1 0 0	XXXX
Line 1	0 1 1 1 1 1 1 0	XXXXXX
Line 2	0 1 0 1 1 0 1 0	X XX X
Line 3	1 1 1 1 1 1 1 1	XXXXXXXX
Line 4	1 0 1 0 0 1 0 1	X X X X
Line 5	1 0 0 1 1 0 0 1	X XX X
Line 6	0 1 0 1 1 0 1 0	X XX X
Line 7	0 1 0 1 1 0 1 0	X XX X
Line 8	0 1 0 0 0 0 1 0	X X

For both the Pac-Man character and the ghosts, the same sprite graphics can be used whether the character is facing left or right. The Atari VCS (like the arcade cabinet) provides a register switch that automatically flips the sprite graphics horizontally. The VCS Pac-Man character always faces to the side—never up or down. If VCS *Pac-Man* were able to look in those two directions, another two sets of three-frame animations would have been needed. Although the arcade board provides a facility for vertical sprite flipping in hardware, the very idea of such mirroring doesn't even make sense on the VCS, as the programmer must manually set up and draw sprites on an individual scan-line basis, not as a bitmap at a Cartesian coordinate.

Sprite graphics take up precious space in ROM. In the VCS *Pac-Man*, each sprite is eight blocks high, requiring eight total bytes to store. The game uses two sprite images for the ghosts—one for their normal state and one for their eaten state. Neither of these includes extra frames for animation. Pac-Man himself animates in three frames when he eats and in six frames when he is touched by a ghost and disappears. All together, that amounts to nine sprites, each one byte wide and eight bytes tall, for a total of 80 bytes used on ROM. This is a modest amount compared to the 192 bytes used for sprite data in *Combat*. By reducing the fidelity of the game's graphics and animation, Frye won back precious ROM space for the additional logic needed to set up the screen and move the ghosts. The need to save ROM points to a major difference between programming *Pac-Man* for an arcade board and programming it for the Atari VCS. The continuous

4K ROM provides greater flexibility than the arcade board, but far less total storage space.

The TIA also provides registers to set sprite colors: one named COLUP0 and the other COLUP1. In many early VCS games, including *Combat*, sprite colors were set once for the entire game. In later games, the program stored a different color value in one or both sprite color registers along with a different bitmap value. Multicolor sprites were implemented, too. These included Pitfall Harry in Activision's *Pitfall!* The careful observer can note color banding in most of these sprite graphics, though, which is not seen in the true bitmapped graphics of later platforms like the NES. This style of "stripe-colored" sprites is a particular trademark of VCS games. Mercifully for Tod Frye, the iconic Pac-Man of the arcade game is a single color, so no further ROM space or horizontal blank logic had to be expended to draw his yellow image convincingly.

Combat uses two sprites, each of which fires a corresponding missile—just what the TIA ordered, or what it was originally ordered to do. But games like Taito's *Space Invaders* were not designed with the peculiarities of the Atari VCS in mind. Sprites were different in many post-1977 arcade games. Most important, there were often more than two per screen! When faced with the rows of aliens in *Space Invaders* or the platoon of ghosts that chases *Pac-Man*, VCS programmers needed to discover and use methods of drawing more than two sprites, even though only two one-byte registers were available.

As discussed in the previous chapter, the TIA offers a set of horizontal motion registers for each of the sprites, the missiles, and the ball. The TIA also exposes another register called HMOVE to execute changes in horizontal motion. These registers were primarily intended to be set during a vertical blank—that is, between screen draws. For example, *Combat* repositions both player and missile horizontal positions each frame, then updates variables in RAM to ensure that the objects are drawn on the appropriate lines, and then updates the horizontal motion registers once at the start of the frame.

Larry Kaplan, one of the first developers to work on the Stella prototype, figured out that sprite data could be reset more frequently than once per frame. Because the VCS requires the program to control every line of the television screen, it is possible to change the sprite graphics' values and their horizontal positions more than once per frame. Kaplan first used this technique in *Air-Sea Battle*, one of the console's launch titles. In the game, multiple rows of enemies, one per row, pass back and forth across the screen. Each player controls a turret on the ground that can be aimed and fired at targets in the air. Multiple targets are presented by resetting the sprite graphics multiple times down the screen. Finally, when it is time to draw the ground, the sprite graphics and horizontal positions are reset for the player turrets.

Another variation of the horizontal movement technique helped bring *Space Invaders* to the system.[5] The trademark feature of the popular arcade game was the armada of slowly descending aliens, arrayed in rows and columns. The TIA, of course, didn't directly support a display of alien forces like this. Kaplan's *Air-Sea Battle* technique allowed multiple sprites to appear down the screen, but *Space Invaders* required multiple sprites in a horizontal line as well. Rick Maurer, the programmer for the VCS port of *Space Invaders*, discovered that strobing HMOVE while a line was being drawn would reposition objects immediately, even if they had already been drawn earlier in that line. The TIA, lacking any memory of what it has already done, begins drawing the data from its sprite graphics registers to the screen any time that HMOVE is reset. After one row of aliens had been drawn using this technique, Maurer had the program read and write new sprite graphics values from ROM to create a new row of aliens. On each row, the aliens could have a different appearance.

These two techniques, combined with the VCS's lack of a frame buffer and subsequent requirement that the programmer draw every scan line, allowed the VCS to overcome the apparent limitation of supporting only two sprites on-screen. Rather than changing both sprites and their positions every frame, one or both could be changed every line. Together, these approaches extended the originally imagined game design space on the Atari VCS, making the unit capable of playing games that were very different from the arcade hits of the mid-1970s. The importance of these exploits was not overlooked at the higher levels of the company. Discussing this technique in 1983, after he had become vice president of product development at Atari, Kaplan commented, "Without that single strobe, H-move, the VCS would have died a quick death five years ago."[6]

Despite the cleverness of these techniques, both vertical positioning and horizontal strobing required that sprites move together in vertical unison, if they were to move vertically at all. Some variations of *Air-Sea Battle* moved different enemy sprites at different rates of speed by writing new values to the horizontal motion registers, but the objects in that case only moved horizontally—never along both horizontal and vertical axes.

Unfortunately, the four *Pac-Man* monsters need to move horizontally and vertically, and to be independent of one another. Nothing like this had been done before on the Atari VCS. Yet, just as *Space Invaders* would have been unrecognizable without its characteristic rows of invaders, so

Pac-Man would have been unrecognizable without its characteristic monster quadruplets.

To draw the four pursuers, programmer Tod Frye relied on a technique called *flicker*. Each of the four ghosts is moved and drawn in sequence on successive frames. Pac-Man himself is drawn every frame using the other sprite graphic register. The TIA synchronizes with an NTSC television picture sixty times per second, so the resulting display shows a solid Pac-Man, maze, and pellets, but ghosts that flicker on and off, remaining lit only one quarter of the time. The phosphorescent glow of a CRT television takes a little while to fade, and the human retina retains a perceived image for a short time, so the visible effect of the flicker is slightly less pronounced than this fraction of time suggests.[7] The fact that the monsters in *Pac-Man* were commonly referred to as "ghosts" apologized somewhat for the flicker and suggested the dimness of an apparition. The manual for the VCS rendition of *Pac-Man* included large illustrations of ghosts to drive the point home. The energizer dots are also comprised of sprite graphics, but they flash regularly, making their visual appearance less odd.

Later ports of games in the *Pac-Man* family, including the 1982 *Ms. Pac-Man* and the 1987 *Jr. Pac-Man*, used less visually intrusive techniques to draw the ghosts. Flicker was employed only when necessary, on one horizontal band of the screen rather than on every frame.

The flicker on the first VCS *Pac-Man* annoyed and disappointed many players. Part of the problem is the nature of human vision. The eyes can simply tire of the constantly flashing ghosts. Another part of the problem is the effect of flicker on gameplay. The flashing of the ghosts makes them harder to see, which is a major problem for a game that is all about pursuit.

Another problem with the visuals is even more subtle. In Iwatani's original game, each ghost has a different color, name, and behavior. This gives each of the opponents at least some sort of personality. The arcade game prominently introduces the monsters by name—Blinky, Inky, Pinky, and Clyde—during attract mode, when the machine is luring players to insert quarters, and Blinky is further fictionalized in the interstitial scenes between levels. No such transfer of characterization was possible on the Atari VCS, in part because the monsters cannot be distinguished from one another.

The flicker technique and the reuse of one sprite also made it necessary to abstract the bonus fruit in the game. Aesthetically, *Pac-Man* is already a very abstract game—even in the arcade. The player eats pellets and energizers, not burgers and cola. The addition of fruit fits the theme

VITAMINS

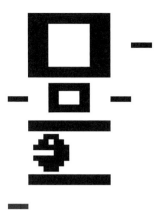

VITAMINS

Vitamins are the two intersecting rectangles in the center of the playfield. They only appear for a few moments and then disappear and reappear. The vitamins are worth 100 points each time PAC-MAN eats them.

4.2 The manual for the VCS *Pac-Man* reimagines the bonus object, which is drawn using playfield graphics, as a "vitamin."

of eating and serves an additional purpose in the game design: considerable bonus points can be earned in return for steering Pac-Man in the right direction to get the fruit. The visual fidelity of these fruits, as well as the incongruity of their appearance, introduces an element of whimsy into the game. Because the maze is identical on each level, the fruit also marks achievement; players would talk about "reaching the apple stage" or "getting to the key" (the nonfruit prize that is offered last) to note their progress and boast about their skill.

To avoid storing even more sprite data in ROM and drawing an additional flickering object that would result in even worse flicker, Frye represented each of the fruit bonuses with a single, even more abstract object: an orange box made of playfield graphics with a yellow player-one missile graphic filling its inside. The object didn't change from level to level as it did in the arcade. In the printed manual for the game, Atari tried to fictionalize this technical decision by calling the bonus object a "vitamin," which was described as "two intersecting rectangles." In this case, the platform constrained the fiction of the game. The image of the vitamin in the manual even looks like a stylized version of the rectangular boxes shown on-screen, as shown in figure 4.2.

Bank Switching and *Ms. Pac-Man*

The VCS version was the first home console port of *Pac-Man*. Atari reportedly produced upwards of ten million cartridges in its first run. This was a very unusual production run, given that there was an active base of only ten million VCS consoles.[8] At the time, Atari executives reasoned that *Pac-Man*'s popularity in the arcade would drive purchases of VCS hardware, thus increasing demand for the game.

However, the cartridge's limitations and compromises led to less than anticipated interest in the game—much less. Atari did sell an impressive seven million copies of the game, but that still left millions to languish in the warehouse or to be returned unsold.[9] This was a massive financial disaster. In the wake of *Pac-Man*'s commercial reception, retailers began to mistrust the videogame industry. Their suspicions would be confirmed with even more licensed games of dubious quality that same year—most prominently, *E.T.: The Extra-Terrestrial*. *Pac-Man* contributed to a chain reaction of reduced retail commitment to home console video games, resulting in the so-called videogame crash of 1983, which is discussed in more detail in chapters 7 and 8. While larger companies like Atari and Activision survived in some form, the many smaller companies producing games for consoles quickly went out of business. It was not until Nintendo released its NES in 1985 that the U.S. videogame market recovered from this dark age.

In the videogame fan world, represented by posts from the Atari amateur community and fan-authored historical documents like Wikipedia's pages on the game, blame for the poor quality of the original VCS *Pac-Man* is leveled squarely at Frye and Atari. Indeed, both programmer and company may have overreached in their attempts to gobble dollars.

Frye developed the game from a prototype that he had been working on when Atari acquired the game rights. The company pressured him to use this incomplete version instead of starting over again so that the game could be released in time for the 1981 Christmas season. Despite the strong technical limitations under which he worked, Frye had an incentive to attempt the best work he could in the space and time he was given. Atari CEO Ray Kassar finally responded to the possibility of Frye and other senior programmers being hired away by offering them a royalty on sales of the cartridges they developed. Frye would get ten cents for every *Pac-Man* unit sold. Once the game shipped and money started rolling on, Frye made no secret of the wealth he was amassing. This didn't endear him to his coworkers, even though they were substantially better off because of the new royalty arrangement.[10] For Atari's part, the company rushed the game to market at the lowest possible cost in order to capitalize on the license alone rather than on a careful, well-crafted rendition of the game.

A year later, Atari released an adaptation of *Ms. Pac-Man* that responded to most of the gripes that players had about VCS *Pac-Man*. Part of this work was derivative of Frye's. Part of it benefited from the perfect hindsight of the original VCS *Pac-Man* debacle.

For one thing, the game used an 8K ROM instead of the 4K ROM that Frye was allotted for his project thanks to a technique called *bank-switching*. The 6507 microprocessor used in the Atari VCS featured only thirteen of the sixteen pins available in the 6502. This limitation reduced the total address space of the machine to 8K, of which 4K is devoted to RAM, the TIA, and the RIOT registers. This leaves 4K of address space for cartridge ROM. As *Pac-Man* demonstrates, limitations in ROM space are just as significant as limitations in computation time or RAM. A bank-switched cartridge partly relaxes this constraint, allowing the program to switch between multiple 4K ROM banks.[11]

The *Ms. Pac-Man* arcade game was itself a variation on *Pac-Man*, originally created by General Computing Company as a daughterboard that attached to the Namco *Pac-Man* board. The arcade game changed the appearance and layout of the maze, also adding three new mazes which appear on successive levels. It also revised the monster AI to make the behavior of the four opponents less evidently deterministic, changed the bonus fruit to move and bounce through the maze, and introduced new cut scenes to go with the fiction of Pac-Man's courtship.

The VCS *Ms. Pac-Man* made considerable use of the additional ROM space that bank-switching afforded. More ROM made it possible to have all four mazes in the game. Additional space for sprites allowed *Ms. Pac-Man* to face in all four directions, to feature better animation, and most important, to include game and character logos, bonus fruits, logos, interstitial screens, and an authentic arcade attract loop (figure 4.3).

Fans and historians sometimes point to *Ms. Pac-Man* and later VCS *Pac-Man* hacks and rebuilds as evidence that *Pac-Man* could have been a much better game than it turned out to be. There is, for example, Nukey Shay's revision of Frye's cartridge, which adds credible arcade sounds, revised colors, better sprite graphics, and colored fruit.[12] Shay also tuned the speed and control interaction to better match the arcade. The game includes better renderings of the main eater and of the ghosts, including animated vertical orientations for Pac-Man. And it replaces the cloying VCS *Pac-Man* startup sound with a credible two-voice rendition of *Pac-Man*'s characteristic theme music—a remarkable feat, given the lack of similarity between Atari's sound registers and the *Pac-Man* board's custom three-channel waveform sound generator.

4.3 The VCS *Ms. Pac-Man* has bonus fruit, an attract screen, and other visual features that connect it to its arcade counterpart.

Despite all of this, it doesn't make sense to blame Frye for not accomplishing what Shay did, or to imagine that the VCS *Pac-Man* could have been a better game just because later versions of it were indeed more faithful adaptations. The situation of *Pac-Man*'s development and release was historically unique. The technical affordances of the Atari VCS itself are further bound, at any point in time, to the types of innovation that have already been accomplished on the platform, along with the player response to the previously released titles. Whether or not the videogame crash that hit in force in 1983 could have been averted, there is no question that a better version of *Pac-Man* could have been released in 1982, given the right circumstances. But those circumstances—a combination of intersecting issues in culture, business, and reception—did not arise. Part of that situation was the very intense demand for an adaptation of a hit arcade game in the first place, a possible signal of the cultural shift toward derivatives, licenses, and branded content as the first phase of cross-media consolidation took root.

If there is a general lesson that can be learned from *Pac-Man*'s fate on the Atari VCS, it is the importance of the framing and social context of a property—video game or otherwise—when adapting it for a particular computer platform. The VCS rendition of *Ms. Pac-Man* demonstrates that an artifact with a strong social and cultural context must carry some significant signs of that context into its adaptation. One videogame writer described the VCS game as "a pale imitation of the real thing," noting that "the cut-scenes were gone, the *paku-paku* sound effect was no more, and Iwatani's colorful, appealing graphic design was butchered."[13] Perhaps the most interesting feature of the VCS rendition of *Ms. Pac-Man* is that it includes an authentic arcade attract loop, dramatic interludes, and accurate *Ms. Pac-Man* logos on both the splash screen and the game screen. These features add nothing to the gameplay, but they provide an important frame for it. A home version of *Pac-Man*, it turned out, needed to simulate the arcade experience, with its sounds and video displays meant to draw players from afar, as much as it needed to allow players to pilot a yellow pizza-critter around an abstract maze.

In 1981 *Yars' Revenge* burst forth from Atari, powered by impressive graphics and sound and providing for compelling play. The game was heavily promoted by the company—and its distinctive qualities made it worth promoting. *Yars' Revenge* became Atari's best-selling original cartridge, one that was emblematic of the Atari VCS experience for many players. The story of its development reveals much more about the interplay between arcade and home games. It also shows how development capabilities were further evolving in the early 1980s and how the facilities of the Atari VCS could be built upon to allow for even more effective play in the context of the home.

Though the cartridge offers such eye candy as a scintillating vertical stripe and similar-looking full-screen explosions, *Yars' Revenge* didn't excel on the strength of its graphics alone. The game includes several different elements, each with unique behaviors, necessitating a lengthy description of the rules in the manual. Original as the cartridge was, the *Yars' Revenge* project was initially supposed to be a simple port of a vector graphics arcade game. The programmer went from this starting point toward something with a markedly different look and with significantly changed gameplay. *Yars' Revenge* does have some affinities with its arcade inspiration, but it ended up earning the designation "original." The hit cartridge even became something of a media property itself—at least, more so than any other VCS game by Atari.

Howard Scott Warshaw's first assignment at Atari was the project that would eventually result in *Yars' Revenge*. Initially, he was to port the arcade game *Star Castle*, produced by Cinematronics, to the Atari VCS. As he told an interviewer, "I soon realized that a decent version couldn't be done, so I took what I thought were the top logical and geometric components of *Star Castle* and reorganized them in a way that would better suit the machine."[1] Warshaw's comment reveals how the platform participates in the ecology of game development. The design of *Yars' Revenge* was not entirely determined by the Atari VCS or dropped on the platform by its programmer with no concern for how the system worked. The original idea was to imitate another game, but the capabilities and limitations of the VCS led the developer to create something different: a reorganization of *Star Castle*'s major components that recognized the differences between vector and raster graphics, exploited the abilities of the TIA, and was well-suited to home play.

Warshaw explained in another interview how radical it was for Atari to drop *Star Castle*, which it had already arranged to license:

> I did something no one else had ever done, I went to my boss and said that I had an idea for an original game that would use the same basic play principles of *Star Castle* but was designed to fit the VCS hardware so it wouldn't suck. And to their credit, they let me go with it. Think about that. They blew off a license to let me pursue an original concept with the promise of making a better game for the system. That would never happen today.[2]

An arcade game that was a hit would of course have a following already, one that might generate enthusiasm and an initial market. Even in the early days, when the arcade hits were *Pong* and *Tank* rather than *Pac-Man*, an arcade game's fan following could be important when it came to the home console market. Seen in this way, the licensed arcade game was not very different from a book or movie, which could also supply a video or computer game with valuable recognition and a ready market of fans.

Even if an arcade game hadn't been a huge success, as was the case with *Star Castle*, it would often be ported. A deployed arcade game contained a complete and fully implemented game design, one that had been tested on the playing (and paying) public. Ironically, however, the hardware capabilities of an arcade machine—in terms of processing power, graphics, and controller setup—were always significantly different from those of the Atari VCS, so that having a well-tested and implemented game design on the arcade platform didn't mean very much when it came to the home console's hardware. A "port" from the arcade to Atari's home system was not like a port from one computer system to another, in which the program being converted would function in the same way on both platforms with only minor differences, after a few small changes were made. For one thing, the VCS code for a game always had to be written from scratch—there was no way to modify and reuse what had been done for the arcade game. As Warshaw explained, "The hardware in coin-ops was way beyond the capability of the VCS and the code frequently wouldn't even have been compatible. The closest to using coin-op technology would be when occasionally we would consult with original coin-op programmers to get questions about AI algorithms answered. The code never even came close to passing from arcade machines to VCS."[3]

Given the differences in platform and the need to rewrite each game from scratch, a port to the Atari VCS had plenty of room to become a fairly involved adaptation rather than a simple re-creation. This could leave some fans of the arcade game disappointed, as happened with *Pac-Man*. It could also lead to the porting project taking a different and interesting turn, as happened when the *Star Castle* project veered off to become *Yars' Revenge*.

The most obvious difference between the *Star Castle* computing system and the VCS was the arcade machine's vector graphics, which Atari called *XY graphics*. Atari's successful arcade games *Tempest*, *Battlezone*, *Asteroids*, and *Lunar Lander* all use this sort of graphics system, which employs a fundamentally different type of monitor. All early arcade games used a CRT, but the ones in vector graphics games are wired differently than are the ones in standard televisions. The electron beam does not sweep across the screen from left to right, being turned on and off as it makes its way down and then returns back to the top sixty times each second. Instead, the electron gun is pointed at a certain location, turned on, and moved from that (x, y) coordinate to another point in a straight line, where it is turned off again. (An oscilloscope functions in a similar way; it just uses a different method of deflecting the electron beam.) Because the beam can be made to move arbitrarily instead of progressively scanning along the screen, this way of illuminating a phosphor-coated screen was also called "random scan." Vector graphics systems draw lines in an (x, y) coordinate system; raster graphics systems draw a grid of bitmap data representing a pattern of pixels.

Cinematronics was the first company to release an arcade game that used this display technology: *Space Wars*, released in 1977. Like the first raster arcade game, Nolan Bushnell's pre-Atari *Computer Space*, it was a two-player arcade implementation of the 1962 PDP-1 program *Spacewar*. *Star Castle* has significantly different gameplay, and was developed by a different person, but the space setting and control scheme show that it is clearly based on Cinematronics' earlier game *Space Wars*.[4]

Vector graphics have certain advantages over raster graphics; at least, they did in the late 1970s and early 1980s. Specifically, it is much easier on a vector system to rotate shapes and to scale them up or down, as is needed when zooming in or out. For instance, to resize an object that is centered on (0,0) and consists of some set of lines, each endpoint's coordinates can simply be multiplied by the scaling factor. It does not get much trickier when the object is centered elsewhere or when there should be different amounts of scaling in the horizontal and vertical axes. It is also straightforward to shear a shape, keeping one axis constant while shifting the other. Rotation, scaling, and shear are the basic linear transformations, and any one can be accomplished by subjecting the coordinates of a shape's points to a single matrix multiplication. In combination with translation (the displacement of the shape in space, which just requires addition of the amount of the displacement), these allow for all the possible transformations that keep straight lines straight.

In a raster graphics system, particularly one with the limited computing power of the Atari VCS, the only feasible way to show a rotation of an object is to display a different bitmap—a hard-coded image of the shape rotated by the desired amount. This is how tanks and planes in *Combat* are rotated, for instance. A simple form of scaling is supported in hardware, via the TIA's number-size registers, but smoother zooming has to be done with new graphics. Even when the display hardware itself is not of the XY graphics sort, these benefits of vector graphics can be seen when comparing software platforms such as an early version of the bitmap-based Macromedia Director and an early version of that company's vector-graphics Flash environment.

Through the Wandering Rocks

Vector graphics games used the special capabilities of the display system to good effect. *Battlezone* is a classic example of a game that uses the scaling capability to make tanks larger, so that they appear to be approaching.

Asteroids, on the other hand, makes more prominent use of the facility for rotating shapes.

Although the ship can move freely about the screen in *Asteroids*, the game is organized radially around the ship, which must be the player's center of attention and which can rotate and fire brilliant shots in all directions. With its space setting, its rotating and firing ship, and its controls, *Asteroids* shares several fundamental qualities with *Spacewar*, with the arcade game *Space Wars*, and also with *Star Castle*. The original arcade *Asteroids*, developed by Ed Logg, is worth comparing to its Atari VCS port, which was published in 1981, as was *Yars' Revenge*.

Brad Stewart, who had earlier done the port of *Breakout* to the Atari VCS after winning the right to port the game by besting a fellow programmer in the arcade *Breakout*, went on to develop the VCS *Asteroids*. Both the VCS and the coin-op game purport to be *Asteroids* and do feature a rotating ship, rocks breaking up into smaller rocks, and flying saucer enemies. But the arcade game uses the capabilities of the vector display beautifully and works well in the situation of the arcade; the cartridge exhibits classic VCS qualities that connect to home gaming traditions and the TIA's affordances.

The arcade *Asteroids* has five buttons that are used as controls during the game: a pair of buttons for rotating clockwise or counterclockwise, a pair to control thrust and fire, and a hyperspace button that is set below the others—exactly the same five buttons as on *Space Wars*. *Star Castle* has controls that are the same except for the hyperspace button, which is missing on the *Star Castle* control panel. In *Asteroids*, the monitor is oriented horizontally and the playing field's topology is that of a torus: objects wrap around vertically and horizontally. This is the same as in *Star Castle*, and is one option that can be selected in *Space Wars*.

A difference between *Star Castle* and the arcade *Asteroids* is the lack of color overlays in *Asteroids*. A monochrome monitor was used for *Asteroids*—originally, the Electrohome G05-801, a 19 monitor made by Wells-Gardner Electronics and previously used in *Lunar Lander*.[5] Without overlays, an image on this monitor appears as white lines on black. The asteroids are drawn more dimly, and move about in arbitrary directions. The ship and flying saucers are drawn more brilliantly, and the shots fired from either are particularly luminous points. These aspects—along with high contrast, sharp lines, and a fast refresh rate—make *Asteroids* visually impressive in a way that is hard to imagine when looking at an emulator, screen shot, or diagram.

The music and sound in the game is simple but very well suited to play, as Sherry Turkle and an arcade game player she interviewed, memorably described: "When the play picks up, *Asteroids* pounds out a beat that stands between a pulse and a drum. 'It's its heartbeat,' says the twelve-year-old player standing next to Marty in the arcade."[6]

A typeface characteristic of vector graphics systems was used for the score, copyright notice, "ASTEROIDS BY ATARI," and the high score list. High scores had been saved and displayed before, initially in pinball games, beginning with Midway's 1976 *Sea Wolf*.[7] But the arcade *Asteroids* introduced an innovation: the ability for a high scorer to enter three initials that are saved and displayed alongside the score. Early games like *Spacewar* and *Pong* could be played only as head-to-head multiplayer games. *Space Invaders* was the first arcade video game to track high scores across individual games, but *Asteroids* was the first game to allow players to personalize a high score with their initials.

This seemingly innocuous feature ushered in a sea change in arcade social practice. On game criticism site GameSpy, the innovation was characterized this way: "*Asteroids* was the first video game to take the idea of multiplayer competition beyond one-on-one challenges that had no consequences beyond the actual players. . . . Players didn't have to play the game together in order to compete with one another, they could compete against a whole community."[8]

High scores built on a tradition that predated the videogame arcade— initials on the board in tavern games like darts, for example—to create a new tradition for the 1980s. Instead of a game played by one person at a time, *Asteroids* became a game played by the whole arcade. In some cases, players competed against friends for rank on the high score list. But more frequently, top score holders were semi-anonymous legends, specters that players would try to top. If they fell just short, they would sometimes deride the person who had scored higher by adding three letters so that the high score list would look like this:

SBJ   23000
SUX   21500

Even though the persistence in *Asteroids* is limited to a set of three-digit codes, the high score list transformed the game from a solitary challenge—man against rock—to a social challenge—player versus player. The space combat gameplay itself became a medium for social combat in the arcade. High score holders felt compelled to return to the arcade to see how their renown had fared in their absence. The goading of the high score screen between *Asteroids* game sessions became important—in some cases, as important as the sessions of space combat that a player personally witnessed.

High score lists in home games served a very different function. Homes are private spaces that don't support chance encounters with known or unknown competitors. High score lists can persist as a tool for personal challenge, a way to leave a mark at a friends house, or (rare in the 1980s) as a place where traces of family activity could be seen. But this kind of high score list would have been limited to the home computer, since home consoles had no internal nonvolatile memory and were not able to save any data to rewriteable cartridge memory until *The Legend of Zelda*. In that cartridge, the feature was used only to save game progress, not to facilitate competition.

In *Yars' Revenge*, no record of the high score is kept, and the score is further deemphasized by being displayed only at the end of levels or when the Yar is destroyed. This gives a pure look to the active game screen, which lacks any numerals or letters and is given over entirely to the playing field, but it also prevents competing players, and the player currently controlling the Yar, from eyeing the score during play.

A player can immediately recognize VCS *Asteroids* as a version of the arcade game. It boasts similar gameplay, visual appearance, and sound. The minor differences are telling, however. The asteroids are filled-in and sometimes flickering masses that are drawn in a few different colors rather than as monochrome outlines.[9] The ship is also solid, and fires at most two shots at once—not the four that are possible in the arcade game. Although emulators have been able to make the VCS *Asteroids* conveniently available on computers, they have also shown sharply blocky pixels which were not seen in the same way by players in the early 1980s. CRT televisions blur pixels together to show something that was clearly different from a vector graphics display, but which is also softer and fuzzier than how it is seen on an LCD display.[10]

Perhaps the most significant difference between arcade and VCS versions is not seen in the graphical display, but felt in how the game operates and how the asteroids move. Rather than moving in arbitrary directions, asteroids on the VCS move mainly up and down with a slight horizontal component to their velocity. This means that staying in the middle of the screen and never using thrust at all can be a very effective strategy in the VCS game. In the arcade game, this style of play gives only the slight advantage of a clearer view.

Asteroids was the first cartridge to use the bank-switching technique discussed earlier in the context of *Pac-Man* and *Ms. Pac-Man*. There was no idea in 1977 that more than 4K—really, more than 2K—would ever be desirable for a VCS cartridge. But as the system took hold in the market and more elaborate projects got under way, engineers at Atari looked into expanding the cartridge's capacity. Larry Kaplan's *Video Chess* was the first cartridge slated to use bank-switched ROM. However, Bob Whitehead managed to revise the game to fit into 4K before it was released in 1979. Stewart worked with Bob Smith at Atari to try to similarly compress *Asteroids*, but the programmers found themselves between a rock and a hard place, unable to fit the game into the largest standard ROM. By this point, Atari had the technology ready to provide more memory: 8K, made of two 4K banks. This was enough, and allowed *Asteroids* to be contained on a cartridge without sacrificing its in-game "heartbeat" music, color asteroids, sixty-six variants for one or two players, and other features.

Building on *Star Castle*

The object of *Star Castle* is to repeatedly destroy the rotating cannon in the center of the screen, with one's triangular, rotating ship, a vessel that looks and moves like the ones in *Asteroids* and *Space Wars*. The enemy cannon appears behind colored overlays and is surrounded by three concentric, rotating shields, each of which is made of line segments. The segments can be destroyed by fire from the player's ship, but whenever an entire ring is shot away, it regenerates. Whenever the player clears a path to the cannon, creating a chance to shoot at it to destroy it, the cannon fires a large missile toward the player's ship. As the player is trying to break down the shield rings, three mines also move out and seek the player's ship. They can be avoided or shot, although shooting them does not increase the score and they soon reappear. After a central cannon is finally successfully destroyed, another one quickly appears with three intact rings around it.

In *Yars' Revenge*, the player's "ship" or "man" is the Yar, a "fly simulator" that is controlled with the joystick. *Yars' Revenge* replaces the pivoting of the ship about a point, which could easily be done by the vector graphics display system of *Star Castle*, with movement in the standard eight directions—up, down, left, right, and diagonally. The latter is a form of movement that was fairly easy for the Atari VCS: translation while facing in one of eight directions. The Yar sprite is animated, requiring an additional frame for each direction, but its appearance facing right is a reflection of what it looks like facing left, allowing for some savings. As was mentioned in the discussion of the VCS *Pac-Man*, up/down reflection is not as straightforward as left/right reflection. For this reason, the Yar sprites for up and down are both laid out in ROM. Switching between the two requires reading a different bitmap. The insect appearance of the Yar was simply based on what Warshaw could draw and animate in an interesting way within a player sprite.[11] The name "Yar" has a more definite referent—it was devised by spelling Atari CEO Ray Kassar's first name backward. Figure 5.1 compares screens from *Star Castle* and *Yars' Revenge*.

The objective in *Yars' Revenge* is the Qotile, which moves up and down along the right side of the screen and is protected by a shield. All of the levels are similar in form, but the first one (and all the odd-numbered levels) have a stationary, somewhat rounded shield around the Qotile, while the other levels (all the even-numbered ones) feature a block of shield whose pieces move left-to-right, down a space, right-to-left, down a space, and then right-to-left again through the block. The motion of the pieces mimics that of the CRT's electron gun as it sweeps across and back while moving down the screen.

Defeating the Qotile is a somewhat complex process. Initially, the Yar is in a mode where it fires shots that can chip away at the shield; it can also directly touch the shield to eat away at it, although eating a block may take several tries. In most variants, when the Yar successfully eats a chunk of shield, the Zorlon Cannon appears and the game enters a different mode. The cannon is the only weapon that can defeat the Qotile. Pressing the button after the cannon has appeared fires it. Complicating matters further are several other game elements. There is a single destroyer missile that, like the three mines in *Star Castle*, seeks the Yar and can kill it. A feature not in *Star Castle* is the stripe of neutral zone; the Yar is safe from the destroyer missile in this zone, but is unable to fire and is not protected from a more powerful attack in which the Qotile fires itself off in the form of a swirl. The swirls are similar to the large missiles that the *Star Castle* cannon fires when a path is cleared to it, but they take off at random. Finally, the Zorlon Cannon, although it is a weapon at the player's disposal, has the ability to hit and kill the player and can even rebound off the shield to do so in certain variants.

On top of all this, the game's behavior changes further in other variants: difficulty increases in three phases as score increases, a large bonus is offered for shooting the Qotile in swirl form, and a larger bonus can be earned for shooting the swirl once it has launched. The first two game variants are easier one- and two-player versions suitable for young children. Two-player hotseat play and one-player play is provided for each of the different difficulty levels. The complex, intertwined objectives and obstacles of *Yars' Revenge* certainly show how far video games had come since *Pong*'s "avoid missing ball for high score."

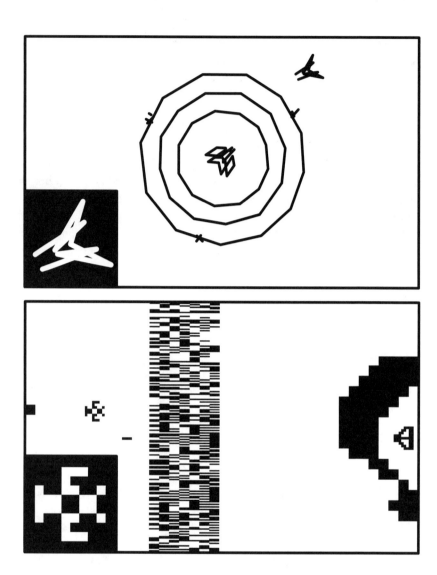

5.1 At top, a screen from *Star Castle*, a vector graphics coin-op game. The screen at the bottom is from *Yars' Revenge*, the Atari VCS cartridge that was inspired by *Star Castle*. Details of the players' ships are inset in each screen, showing signs of the different display technologies that are being used.

There are reasons for these intricacies that cannot be attributed solely to the programmer's whim. Because there is only one button on the VCS joystick, it is impossible to map one button to one type of weapon and another button to another, even though this type of setup was common on arcade games of the time—*Tempest* offered superzappers, *Defender* smartbombs. It was not an option to have one button for the Zorlon Cannon and one for regular firing. Instead, *Yars' Revenge* has two different modes. In one, the button shoots the typical ordnance from the Yar, the energy missile; in the other, the button fires the Zorlon Cannon, which follows the Yar horizontally but is fixed to launch from the far left of the screen.

Although it might seem that complexity of this sort would inhibit new players, testing didn't indicate any problems along these lines, and neither did sales. There are a few reasons why the nature of the game may not have put off new players. Cartridges were a costly investment, so any player who purchased the game was likely to check the manual out in some detail before declaring the game a dud. Players of the early 1980s would be more likely to read manuals for other reasons. Today's players expect the game to teach them how to play, step by step, with live on-screen instruction via pointers and overlays. The Atari VCS has no built-in support for text rendering, and no programmer would have thought to waste precious ROM space with instructions. Instead, this aspect of the experience was offloaded to the manual. Most VCS cartridges also included many variants—*Combat*'s twenty-seven video games, for example. To understand which variant was which, the player would have to consult a chart or description in the manual. An obvious fact that is nevertheless worth noting is that there was no World Wide Web in 1981, and the dial-up computer bulletin board services (BBS) had not yet become popular, so checking online to find out how to play wasn't an option.

But it wasn't always necessary for players to consult the manual to learn a game's intricacies. They could learn from someone else who had figured out how to play—even if that person hadn't completely mastered the game or understood every detail. The complexity of play, rather than always shutting out newbies, sometimes offered an opportunity for those who had played a bit to discuss how the game worked. This sense of experimentation has not been entirely lost in contemporary video gaming, although times have certainly changed.

To continue pursuing the details of this game's workings, consider the two options for attacking the shield. A player can eat away at it by bringing the Yar directly into contact with it or fire at it from farther away. This dual approach allows expert players to chew away in more risky but higher-scoring maneuvers, while less skilled players can choose the easier option of attacking the shield from a distance. Players can hide from the missile in the neutral zone, avoid it, or, if they like, shoot at it. The neutral zone can be a pleasant refuge, but as it does no good against the Qotile's swirl, it does not provide a defense against every attack.

Killing a Qotile with a missile as it moves up and down along the right side of the screen is a fine accomplishment, and earns the player a thousand points, a substantial amount compared to the sixty-nine points earned by shooting away a single part of the shield. If the Qotile has transformed into a swirl and remains along the right side of the screen, the bounty increases to two thousand points. The real payoff comes from hitting a swirl that has launched into the air against the player. This nets the player six thousand points and an extra life. As with shooting the shield (as opposed to eating it), this method provides more capable players with an additional challenge while letting others progress and earn fewer points.

Beyond the basic redesign of the gameplay and the graphical advances that were made, there were a few other innovations—minor, but telling—in *Yars' Revenge*. These features show how game software could allow a fixed hardware platform to evolve and suit the needs of home players a bit better. They include the ability to reset the game from the joystick without reaching over to the console and using the reset switch, a convenience that would evolve into the NES's placement of select and start buttons on the controller itself. Another first was an "official" Easter egg. Robinett had slipped his name into *Adventure* without permission; Warshaw got marketing to agree to let him code the game so that his initials would appear when the Yar is navigated to a certain spot on the explosion screen.

Yars' Revenge also has a makeshift but useful facility for pausing the game. The program waits at the beginning of each new level for the player to press the button, allowing gamers to take a break from a play session and to return to continue playing. There were some similar features in other games, such as *Breakout*, which waits for the player to press the paddle button to serve the ball. This contrasted with how the ball serves automatically in the original *Pong*. The inclusion of this feature helped players overcome the Atari VCS's lack of a true pause button and acknowledged the difference between arcade games and home video games. In the arcades, it was imperative to drive players through short games in order to harvest additional quarters from them—no concept of pausing is compatible with coin operation. At home, companies were competing to have players purchase more cartridges. Long game sessions were perfectly consistent with this goal, as they still are today.

Yars' Revenge features a large, four-part video kernel. There is one part to draw the swelling explosion that ends a level, another to display the score, another to draw the shield for half the frames of the main sequence, and a final one to draw, in alternating frames during the main sequence, the multicolored neutral zone.

The neutral zone's random-looking patterns are not provided by a pseudorandom number generator—an intricate algorithm that, although deterministic, is complex enough to create a sequence that looks random. Such an algorithm can be implemented on the Atari VCS (as is discussed in relation to *Pitfall!* in the next chapter), but it exacts a price in ROM (the code itself must be stored somewhere) and in cycles (the code must be run while the game is also carrying out the work of drawing the screen and updating the game state). The alternative is to lay out a random-looking pattern in ROM and simply load random-seeming bytes from this small entropy pool, one that suffices to create a disorganized visual display. This approach takes fewer cycles, but it requires that some random-looking pattern, perhaps a fairly large one, is stored in ROM. If such a pattern were to be added, something else in the game would have had to give— there are fewer than a handful of bytes free in the finished *Yars' Revenge*.

Warshaw used the second technique, but he made use of a random-looking sequence of bytes that would already be laid out in ROM by the time the game was finished—the game's code itself:[12]

```
EOR (neutralZonePtr),Y
AND neutralZoneMask
STA PF2
AND #$F7
STA COLUPF
```

In this part of the neutral zone kernel (the first instruction is located at $F084), the values pointed to by neutralZonePtr are brought into the accumulator and masked against the contents of neutralZoneMask. This accumulator value is used first as the pattern that is loaded into a playfield register and, after it is masked again, as the playfield color. The label neutralZonePtr points to the same address as does another label, game-Timer. At this location, a count is stored that is continually incremented, once each line, and ranges over the addresses in cartridge ROM. This progression works it way through the code of the *Yars' Revenge* cartridge, with each byte of code being loaded, transformed, and displayed on the screen. The bytes in ROM end up being used in three contexts: as executable code, as playfield graphics, and as the playfield color. When the Qotile is hit, they also supply the random-looking arrangement of the full-screen explosion.

Warshaw told an interviewer that he had planned to use this method from the start rather than working it out as a solution to a problem that came up: "It was just a cheap way to get the effect I wanted. I didn't have the time or space to do it any other way."[13] Still, by making the game's code into an important visual component of *Yars' Revenge*, Warshaw showed how a functioning program could shine aesthetically. When the player looks at the neutral zone on the screen, he is also literally looking at the code. *Yars' Revenge* may not have had any direct influence on the spectacular movie *Tron* released the summer after the game, but the multicolored Master Control Program is cast in a different light by the neutral zone, actually drawn again and again by its own image, a liminal code-and-data Janus.

Into Fiction; On to the Future

In *Yars' Revenge*, the unique nature of the game elements, the possibility for one's ship to both fire and eat away at a shield, and the unusual shape of the ship also offered hooks to which other fictional media could attach. The comic *Yars' Revenge: The Qotile Ultimatum* was included with the cartridge, something that might not have worked as well with early titles such as *Combat*, *Air-Sea Battle*, or *Video Olympics*. At any rate, no similar comic projects seem to have been considered early in the system's history.

There was also a *Yars' Revenge* album for children, released under the Kid Stuff Records label, as well as an Atari-licensed Yar Halloween costume. There was even some discussion during the original VCS game's development of doing an arcade version of *Yars' Revenge*. A VCS-to-arcade port never became a reality, but the very idea was probably unprecedented. From the origins of the Atari VCS until the early 1980s, it was always assumed that arcade games would supply the titles and game designs for VCS games, and it was almost never imagined that innovation might move in another direction.

Yars' Revenge programmer Howard Scott Warshaw went on to program two other important VCS cartridges: *Raiders of the Lost Ark* and *E.T.: The Extra-Terrestrial*. These high-profile, prize projects were attempts to capitalize on films, and were part of a trend that is discussed in chapter 7 alongside the VCS game *Star Wars: The Empire Strikes Back*. Both of Warshaw's later games were quite different from *Yars' Revenge*, favoring exploration over shooting and fast action. In addition to a Nintendo Game Boy

Color port of *Yars' Revenge* in 1999, there was also, oddly enough, a VCS sequel to the game developed more than twenty years after the original and released as part of the Atari Flashback 2 TV game system in 2005.

The multicolored neutral zone, pulsing color and sound, hi-res score, proto-pause feature, and repeating but intricate gameplay of *Yars' Revenge* clearly came about in the context of how little the Atari VCS was able to do—and how much it could manage when it was pushed. Certainly, the cartridge looks primitive when compared even to the typical NES game. It looks much more so when lined up against later 3D games. But when compared to the VCS launch titles, *Yars' Revenge* can be seen as making a significant advance in graphics, sound, gameplay, and interface. It also shows how an arcade game could be reimagined as a home "original." Perhaps this VCS cartridge didn't step up to the level of *Super Mario Bros.* or *The Legend of Zelda*, but for its moment—closer to the late-1977 *Combat* than to the late-1985 *Super Mario Bros.*—it was a considerable accomplishment.

Warshaw himself is clearly proud of the game's status as a bag of tricks that introduced many novel features and Atari VCS firsts, but he finds the integrated experience of the game and its highly playable nature and widespread appeal to be its biggest achievement: "What was most exciting to me was to have made my first game be a significant debut and make a splash. That and making a game that was good enough that I enjoyed playing it. I was very proud of all that was achieved by *Yars*. Although, if I had to pick one thing, it might be that it was that *Yars* scored highest among adult women, the single hardest market segment to reach."[4]

We, too, are unable to locate the secret of this game's success in any one technical feature. But there is another quality of *Yars' Revenge*, beyond its playability, that bears mentioning: the game's unusual visual, aural, and interactive aesthetic. If members of today's generation of gamers were to walk in and see a game of *Yars' Revenge* in progress on a screen, they might be unlikely to praise the graphics and sound, but they would likely be startled by the unusual image and look twice at it. This game does not fill the screen with cleverly duplicated sprites, as was typical in the shoot-em-up genre. And it does not use the saturated colors that would become typical of Activision games. There is no score display during the main sequence of play. The pulsing Qotile sprite and the blocky shield of subdued color are a great contrast to the multicolored, shimmering stripe that seems to rupture the display straight through to the level of code.

The sound in *Yars' Revenge* was effective at the time—and elements of it were, in many ways, quite typical of videogame sound and music in 1981. To some, the background droning may have sounded similar to, and about as compelling as, the "heartbeat" of *Asteroids*. But it was also not too far removed from the tank-tread grinding and background hum of *Combat*. The sonic landscape of the game was not constructed from any sort of complex interactive musical score—music during gameplay was not typical on the Atari VCS. Rather, it was built up from intermittent sound effects overlaid on or replacing the background drone. This rough droning might have evoked to period game players the overall hum of activity and the blending sounds of coin-op games at the arcade. But even if it was familiar in some ways, the sound had its own unusual qualities, hovering somewhere between noise and music.

The subgenre of shooter into which *Yars' Revenge* falls would have to be that of the fixed or single-screen shooter, a category which also includes the arcade games *Space Invaders*, *Galaxian*, *Phoenix*, *Centipede*, and *Gorf*, all of which were ported to the Atari VCS; *Galaga*, a famous game that wasn't ported to the system; and *Demon Attack*, an original game published by Imagic for the Atari VCS. But *Yars' Revenge* differs from all of these games by having the main axis of conflict oriented horizontally rather than vertically. This unusual choice, and the numerous modes and complexities of play, mean that *Yars' Revenge* plays in a way that is as strange, and as oddly pleasing, as it looks and sounds.

Although *Yars' Revenge* was off-kilter in many interesting ways, it was dead on as a VCS cartridge, making use of the sound, graphics, and interface that the system was best at providing. The full-screen explosion and eight-directional Yar would have made no sense in the context of an XY graphics system. Similarly, it would have been bizarre in the extreme for *Yars' Revenge* to have come about on the competing Intellivision. The Qotile and Yar, represented with the two VCS player sprites, would have been less natural as lone antagonists on that platform, which featured eight moving objects. There would be no need for the special mode for firing the Zorlon Cannon, as the Intellivision controller has two fire buttons, not to mention a keypad. And, to avoid giving the false impression that the Intellivision was technically superior in every way and was a simple superset of the Atari VCS, nothing like the fading and reappearing of the Qotile and the shimmering of the neutral zone would have been possible using the frame-buffered sixteen-color graphics system of that console.

Warshaw's "original" was a brilliant variation on *Star Castle*, played in virtuoso style on the Atari VCS. His skill in creating *Yars' Revenge* is not just seen in his programming chops and creativity. It can also be found in his ability to innovate and improvise while building down from the top (an already completed vector graphics coin-op game with a working game mechanic), and up from the bottom (a platform that offered a particular set of affordances and was used in the context of the home). Many creative computational works are based on earlier programs to some extent, either very directly (as with the VCS *Pac-Man*), with some modification and extension *(Combat)*, with more radical reorganization *(Yars' Revenge)*, or with a complete change of display, interface, and paradigm *(Adventure)*. But whatever the influence of past programs, the developer always also encounters the current platform. When the work being developed is innovative, it is often enabled by new exploration of a platform's capabilities, by reconceptualizing the platform's limitations, and by attending in new ways to how and why people use it. *Yars' Revenge* is clever code, but the cartridge really excels when seen in the context of Atari's early VCS games and when plugged into its platform to be enjoyed by players.

For a third-party home videogame developer in the early 1980s, the terrain was loaded with treasures, laced with traps, and entirely unknown. It was in this context that the upstart company Activision ran ahead to develop and market the 1982 cartridge *Pitfall!* by David Crane. The game held the top spot on the Billboard charts for 64 consecutive weeks and helped establish more than one videogame genre.

Third-Party Games from Activision

David Crane, Larry Kaplan, Alan Miller, and Bob Whitehead were Atari's star programmers in the late 1970s, although this wasn't obvious to them until a memo was distributed with sales figures for VCS games. Crane tallied up his titles—they were pretty much his; although Atari packaged and sold them, he had done everything on them from concept through design to programming and in-game art and sound, as was always in the case in those days. Crane found that the cartridges he developed (*Outlaw, Canyon Bomber,* and *Slot Machine*) had earned more than $20 million for the company. As he said, "I was one of the people wondering why I was working in complete anonymity for a $20,000 salary."[1] Others began to feel the same:

When we looked closely at that memo, we saw that as a group we were responsible for 60 percent of their $100 million in cartridge sales for a single year," Crane recalled. "With concrete evidence that our contribution to the company was of great value, we went to the president of Atari to ask for a little recognition and fair compensation. Ray Kassar looked us in the eye and said, 'You are no more important to Atari than the person on the assembly line who puts the cartridges in the box.' After that it was a pretty easy decision to leave."[2]

Atari was not the same company that it had been under founder Nolan Bushnell. Although there had been a change, the idea of radical equality Kassar cited in response to Crane's request—programmer being equal to assembly line worker—had a precedent. In the early days, Bushnell maintained a policy that no one would be fired (although they might be denied a raise) and ensured that everyone, from executives to assembly line workers, had the same health care plan. But with VCS development organized along a model of the lone programmer who was almost completely, individually responsible for a sometimes very lucrative game, it became less tenable to claim that the programmer was no more important than any other human resource.

Crane and Miller had the good fortune to meet Jim Levy, who was already seeking venture capital and working toward starting a software business. They joined him to found Activision in 1979. Kaplan and Whitehead followed soon after. Levy, who had worked as a recording industry executive, was ready to build up the image of programmers and present them to the game-buying public as individuals with personalities. Activision used means that already existed—manuals, boxes, and advertisements—to promote the programmers. At the same time, the company created a distinctively non-Atari corporate identity, using only the most saturated colors in its games, developing a consistent, distinct style for labels and boxes, and including the Activision logo (but not any programmers' names) on every game screen. See figure 6.1 for an example of an Activision box.

Convincing investors of the value of a venture like Activision was not easy, but the most substantial barrier for any third-party VCS publisher was the proprietary nature of the Atari VCS. Later companies would have to reverse-engineer the platform to learn anything about how to program it. Activision had the advantage of starting with four ex-Atari programmers who were already conversant with the Atari VCS. Atari did what it could to dissuade Activision from going into business, which included filing a lawsuit against the company in 1980 that alleged copyright violations and trademark infringement. It was not settled until 1982, when third-party development of VCS cartridges had become firmly entrenched.

6.1   The box art for Atari's VCS launch title *Indy 500*, shown on the top left, features an intricate, realistic painting of the game's subject. The game itself is much more abstract, as an image of the screen on the bottom left shows. The box art for David Crane's early Activision title *Grand Prix*, top right, more closely matches the level of abstraction and even the aesthetic used in the game itself, as seen on the screen on the bottom right.

From an economic standpoint, Atari took a tremendous hit by losing its lock on profit-making cartridges. But it's not clear that Activision was entirely bad news for Atari. As both Activision and Atari programmers have recently suggested, the new source of competition may have ended up goading Atari programmers to develop better games.[3]

Development Practices

Today, video games are usually created by large teams working for many years on a single project. The largest games require teams of several hundred people. These teams are divided into strict roles: programmer, artist, voice actor, designer, producer. In the heyday of the Atari VCS, a single programmer would create an entire game. Until Imagic broke the mold by having artist Michael Becker create the in-game graphics for its 1982 *Demon Attack*, an "artist" working in game development was the person who illustrated the box art or designed the game's printed manual.[4]

One might imagine that VCS games were created by one individual just because they were simple. But as the previous chapters suggest, the machine was anything but simple to program. In the early days of the Atari VCS, though, software engineering for microcomputers and videogame consoles was not nearly as industrialized a practice as it is now. Commercial software was usually developed by individuals or small groups. For example, in 1981, Microsoft bought exclusive rights to its first Disk Operating System (DOS) from an individual coder and then licensed it to IBM.[5]

Although it is possible for VCS programmers to share code, cartridge development for the system is not amenable to the engineering of individual titles by large teams. Even though programmers learned each other's techniques (both by directly talking to one another and by reverse-engineering what others had done), their work did not divide into neatly reusable subroutines. This does not mean that VCS programs were under-engineered or poorly written—the precise timing required just to get the screen to draw wouldn't allow for much sloppiness in coding. But the constraints of ROM and RAM usage, cycle timing, and logic timing often demanded unusual and unintuitive shortcuts.

For example, in the early days of Activision, programmers would push up against various boundaries. They would often run out of ROM space. Most 6502 assembly instructions are two bytes: one for the opcode and one for the operand. Saving space on ROM requires consolidating code—usually removing one line for every two bytes of space reclaimed.

Assembler programs are composed of elementary instructions, not of higher-order functions. For example, the following assembly language instructions load a value from the top of RAM, add the value 8 to it, and store the result in the TIA register that sets the background color:

```
LDA $80
ADC #$08
STA COLUBK
```

Each of the opcodes (LDA, ADC, and STA, in this case) are mnemonic shortcuts for one-byte hexadecimal values that tell the processor what operation to execute. The opcode LDA, for instance, loads a value into the processor's accumulator, a special register in which it can perform mathematical operations. When assembled into machine code, the opcode mnemonic "LDA" becomes the hexadecimal value A9. Here is what the three example lines look like in machine code:

A9 80 69 08 85 09

ROM frugality often required clever rearrangements of assembler code, which sometimes made the resulting source files appear to be puzzles encrypting their content rather than roadmaps elucidating it.

Consider a characteristic example. In an attempt to recover ROM space, Bob Whitehead moved one of his subroutines so that it ended just before a block of sprite data. The TIA's sprite registers hold only a single byte of data at a time, which the program changes each on scan line. In this case, the first line of the sprite data was the hexadecimal value $60, which also happens to be the machine reference for the opcode RTS (return from subroutine). In this code, then, the value $60 serves two purposes, as the opcode RTS when it is encountered in program flow and as the value $60 (binary %01100000) when it is read as data. As with the rendering of the *Yars' Revenge* neutral zone, this is an example of the use of the contents of ROM—only a single byte, in this case—as both code and data.

Examples like this one show the subtlety of trade-offs sometimes necessary to make a VCS cartridge producible. Particular compromises would include the removal of features from the game. But in this case, the visual design of an on-screen object was subject to an aesthetically unrelated happenstance, the accident of a processor instruction used for program flow control.

By the early 1980s, VCS development was still largely the same, although some changes were brewing. At Atari and Imagic, the first artist-programmer teams were created, allowing artists to focus on sprite and screen visuals. Almost all of Activision's founders were successful VCS programmers with a refined technical knowledge of the machine as well as an intimate understanding of the commercial viability of their talents. Instead of isolating its developers in backrooms as Atari had done, Activision created "design centers": small, close-knit teams of four to five people working together. Activision's original four formed the Pasadena

Design Center. The company later added the East Coast Design Center and the Boston Design Center.

The work environment was more atelier than software shop. Developers worked together in large rooms, occasionally turning to each other to discuss design or programming techniques. David Crane told the story of one such discussion: Carol Shaw was hard at work on *River Raid*, which would become an influential vertical scrolling shooter. In the game, the player has to maintain the plane's fuel supply, flying it over canisters in the river. There is a detailed fuel gauge at the bottom of the screen, but Shaw wanted to include audio feedback as well. She was programming alongside several other Activision developers, and she asked for advice on an appropriate klaxon-style sound to warn the player when the fuel level became dangerously low. According to Crane, he rolled back in his chair, looked up in thought for a moment, and recited a few lines of assembly code that created the effect perfectly.[6]

Activision particularly encouraged peer review, the sharing of prototypes, and even critiques of games in progress. These interactions resulted in a major change to *Pitfall!* in the final week of development. Just before the game was to be released, the version that was running offered the player only one life for the whole game, not the three that were provided in the final cartridge. In typical Crane fashion, he imagined that giving the player one life for the whole game would offer the ultimate challenge. "Thankfully," Crane explained, "my buddies practically tied me to my chair until I put in extra lives and I'm glad they did."[7]

Design Philosophies and Styles

By the early 1980s, VCS programmers had moved well beyond the obvious capabilities of the machine. Groundbreaking arcade games including *Space Invaders*, *Pac-Man*, and *Donkey Kong* had come out, putting pressure on VCS development. *Pong* and *Tank* were no longer kings. VCS developers had also grown more fluent in the platform, and they began to push it in new ways with their growing expertise. The change was remarked upon at the time, for instance, in a guide to home video games: "The graphics of the Atari [VCS] games have undergone a metamorphosis. Earlier cartridges produced in the late 1970s reflect more limited computer capacity and programming expertise. Atari graphics have recently become more impressive."[8]

At Activision, noticeably different design philosophies began to develop. For example, Steve Cartwright, the programmer of *Barnstorming* and *Frostbite*, favored iteration and refinement. In his job interview at

Activision, Cartwright suggested a possible variant to Bob Whitehead's popular *Skiing* cartridge.[9] If the skier were changed to a kayaker, he surmised, the interaction could remain largely the same, but would allow for adjustments to the setting and refinements in the character's behavior. This sort of technique would later come to be known as *skinning*. Today, the term has a negative connotation, suggesting commercial exploitation without fundamental innovation. But Cartwright's design philosophy was not without its positive qualities. It involved the slow refinement of basic ideas toward perfection.

Cartwright's first Activision game was *Barnstorming*, released in 1981.[10] In it, the player to navigates a biplane through barns while avoiding obstacles. The player controls the plane with the joystick, which is seen from the side. In 1982, Cartwright created *Seaquest*, a submarine combat game. The player controls a vessel once more, this time in water, and this time avoiding, collecting, or destroying various objects at different levels of depth. *Frostbite*, Cartwright's next game, was released in 1983 and is similar as well. The player moves the character Frostbite Bailey across a freezing river, taking care to land only on ice floes that move from side to side. As the player changes the colors of these floes, a block of an igloo appears on the icy bank at the top of the screen. *Frostbite* is a very different game from *Barnstorming*, but it retains core behaviors from its predecessors: a player object moves up and down into "lanes" on the screen, avoiding or collecting objects. All of these games clearly take advantage of the line-by-line nature of VCS graphics. As in *Air-Sea Battle* and *Freeway*, nonplayer objects are constrained to specific horizontal patches of the screen, so that the sprite graphics registers can be reset at different vertical locations and more than two simultaneous objects can appear on-screen.

David Crane's design philosophy was quite different from Cartwright's. Crane saw Atari VCS development less as a refinement of the gameplay in known interaction models and more as a challenge to make the highly constrained VCS hardware do new and exciting things. In Crane's words, "I got more enjoyment out of discovering a new trick than from the game design itself. More often than not, I used this technique to lead me in a new direction of game design, and some of the tricks were to me as much an accomplishment as solving the Rubik's Cube the first time."[11]

Freeway, which Crane developed in 1981, offered an improvement on the techniques of same-screen sprite register rewrites (which Larry Kaplan had first used in *Air-Sea Battle*) and multicolored sprites (first used in the 1978 *Superman*) accomplished by changing both the sprite color

(COLUP0/COLUP1) and graphics (GRP0/GRP1) values between scan lines. Although neither technique was new, the two were combined in *Freeway* in a synthetic way, causing many more objects to appear in multiple colors. In the game, each player controls a chicken, which can move up and down across a ten-lane highway. The top and bottom lines of each row of cars appear black to indicate the tires. The rest of the car is drawn in a single, solid color, with blank areas forming the window glass. The effect is extremely simple, yet disarmingly effective. The tank sprites in *Combat* and the car sprites in *Indy 500* certainly resemble the objects they are supposed to indicate, but the addition of black tires and windscreens makes *Freeway*'s vehicles feel more like cars and less like icons of cars. Additional background detail, including lane dividers drawn with playfield graphics, also work to create a realistic sense of the location.

Grand Prix, a side-scrolling racing game that Crane created in 1982, is another interesting case. There had been previous racing games for the system, including the 1977 launch title *Indy 500* and Robinett's *Slot Racers*, but these games had tracks that appeared on single screens. *Grand Prix* scrolls from right to left and includes computer-controlled cars that the player must avoid. To accomplish this, Crane had to find a way to draw cars entering and exiting the screen on either side. In a modern buffered graphics system, this is a rudimentary problem: the programmer simply positions a bitmap graphic so that it crosses the edge of the screen. But the TIA automatically wraps sprite graphics from right to left. Positioning a competitor car at one edge of the track would make a portion of the sprite, which should not be displayed, appear on the other edge. Crane could have scrolled the game vertically, but this was not as suitable for drawing large, realistic-looking, multicolored vehicles.

Changing the color of a sprite between horizontal lines, as in *Freeway*, is relatively easy. But changing colors from color clock to color clock across the screen is more or less impossible. Loading a color value from ROM and storing it in one of the sprite graphics registers requires a minimum of six processor cycles, while the TIA traces three color clocks for every *single* cycle of the processor. In the time it takes to load and store a single color value, the TIA will have drawn an area nine "pixels" in length.

To accommodate richly colored cars that don't wrap around the screen, Crane had to keep track of the competitor car positions relative to the edges. If a car needed to hang off either side, instead of drawing the whole sprite, Crane drew only the portion of the car necessary to reach the edge of the screen. Of course, this also meant that separate sprite graphics, one for each possible horizontal slice of the vehicle, had to be stored in ROM—doing computation to crop sprites on the fly was not practical. More than just a little geekery motivated Crane's design philosophy; it was partly driven by a desire to master the machine and show up his colleagues. Crane explains in a 1983 interview in *TWA Ambassador* magazine, "It was unthinkable before that to make a car the shape and color of those in *Grand Prix*. At the time I was doing *Grand Prix*, people were telling me there was no way to pack that much information into the limited amount of memory space we had available. So I did. So there!"[12]

Crane's games also drew largely on his own experiences or interests rather than licensed properties or previous designs. In the case of *Freeway*, Crane had seen a man trying to run across Chicago's Lake Shore Drive during rush hour, and it occurred to him that the challenge would be particularly appropriate for the Atari VCS—running across a freeway brings a whole new meaning to *collision detection*. An early prototype of *Freeway* features little men instead of chickens.[13] In this version, contact with a car results in a shimmering puddle of blood on the road. Reflecting on creatures that cross the road—and perhaps recalling the *Death Race* controversy, described in the next chapter—Crane changed the man to a chicken. In the version of *Freeway* that finally shipped, collisions push the chickens back two lanes rather than crushing them.

Pitfall! Crosses the Road

Pitfall! is an important early platformer and a predecessor to the side scroller, a form of video game that was made famous by *Super Mario Bros.* In this form, the "man" is seen from the side and typically moves from left to right as the background and structures continuously appear on the right and disappear on the left. *Pitfall!* is a platformer, but not a true scroller. Because a new screen appears when the character is moved to the edge of the screen, the cartridge is more of a "pager," like *Adventure*. But unlike *Adventure*, *Pitfall!* is a "side pager," with a perspective that catches the avatar in profile rather than above. In this regard, it is more similar to *Superman*. With its side view, the ability of Pitfall Harry to jump, swing, and climb and fall between different levels, and with the need to drive this character horizontally toward treasures, *Pitfall!* was an exciting early specimen of the genre and managed to do a great deal without smoothly scrolling.

A man crossing the highway inspired *Freeway*, but *Pitfall!* arose from a combination of multiple influences, both technical and cultural. It started with the challenge of creating realistically animating graphics on the Atari VCS. The sprites in early games were static—one graphic comprises *Combat*'s planes, *Slot Racers*' cars, even *Superman*'s multi-colored human characters. Crane had already experimented with simple animation to great effect in *Grand Prix*, giving the cars wheels with tire treads that spin at different rates depending on the car's speed. But he had previously sketched out an idea for a realistically moving man. This became the basis for Pitfall Harry.

Because of the limitations of RAM, ROM, and processor cycles that were inherent to VCS programming, graphics like sprites were not considered external assets that could be dropped into a game. VCS programmers used quad-ruled paper to sketch out designs for sprites, considering not only the eight-bit-wide patterns needed to render a subject convincingly, but also how to design without changing sprite colors during a scan line and while accounting for the total size of a set of sprites in ROM. In some cases, the possible locations of a sprite on-screen would dictate whether color changes were possible—for example, there might not be enough time to change sprite color and graphics values in addition to playfield graphics.

Another issue was the legibility of sprite graphics on-screen. The eight-bit width of VCS sprites doesn't provide a lot of room for detail, and some objects or creatures prove very difficult to render in such low resolution. Crane explained, "Early in my career at Atari, I designed a *Slot Machine* game. When I tried to draw traditional slot machine symbols—cherries, lemons, oranges, etc.—it became clear that there was no way to render those objects in 8 monochrome pixels. So I used cactus, cars and other angular objects that were easily recognizable when drawn with pixels."[14] The choice of the scorpion and cobra obstacles in *Pitfall!* evolved from a similar process, motivated more by how convincingly these opponents could be rendered than by any prior interest in those creatures.

Crane worked on the "little running man" animation for several months, refining its appearance and behavior.[15] He walked deliberately around the office, trying to record his own leg and arm positions and to translate those movements to pixel paper. However, Crane didn't do anything with the little running man right away. Each time he finished a project, he would bring out the designs and think about a game that might make good use of it. Finally in 1982, a plan came together:

> I sat down with a blank sheet of paper and drew a stick figure man in the center. I said, "OK, I have a little running man. . . . Let's put him on a path" (two more lines drawn on the paper). "Where is the path? . . . Let's put it in a jungle" (draw some trees). "Why is he

running? . . . (draw treasures to collect, enemies to avoid, etc.) And *Pitfall!* was born. This entire process took about 10 minutes. About 1000 hours of programming later the game was complete.[16]

The inspiration for *Pitfall!* wasn't the side-scrolling jungle adventure, but rather the running man. The adventure just gave him a reason to run.

Cultural Inspiration

Today, highly detailed videogame characters with complex backstories are common. Miyamoto's Jumpman (who later became Mario) and Iwatani's Pac-Man had become cultural icons before *Pitfall!* was released. But Pitfall Harry was the first popular videogame character born on a home console system. He eventually spawned numerous sequels, licensed products, and even a television cartoon. The little running man was partly responsible, but cultural references also helped fully furnish the game's fictional world.

The film *Raiders of the Lost Ark* was released in 1981. Crane acknowledges that the movie inspired the idea for an adventure in the jungle. But apart from that particular kind of wilderness setting and a guy who runs, little about his game resembles *Raiders*. (Howard Scott Warshaw's official Atari VCS *Raiders of the Lost Ark* cartridge takes considerable license with the film's character and the plot, but nevertheless has many more identifiable elements that can be read as related to the film.) Beyond the cinematic adventure of Indiana Jones, there were two important inspirations that contributed to Crane's design.

The first explains Pitfall Harry's ability to swing on a vine. This idea, of course, comes from Tarzan, the original vine-swinger, who was created by Edgar Rice Burroughs in 1912.[17] Tarzan also inspired Taito's 1982 arcade game *Jungle Hunt*, although that game was developed independently of *Pitfall!*, with neither developer knowing about the other project.[18] Perhaps jungle fever was in the air in that year.

The second explains the crocodiles in some of the *Pitfall!* ponds. From the 1940s through the mid-1960s, Paul Terry's Terrytoons studio, best known for the character Mighty Mouse, released a theatrical cartoon series featuring two magpies named Heckle and Jeckle. The cartoons featured typical amusing pranks, in which the two birds calmly outwitted a variety of foes. In one sequence, the two ran across the heads of crocodiles, deftly escaping their snapping jaws. Crane, who was born in the mid-1950s, remembered seeing the cartoons as a child. He speculated that this idea would make an interesting mechanic in an adventure game.[19]

The result was interesting indeed, partly thanks to how it made the Heckle and Jeckle maneuver interactive. To the amateur player of *Pitfall!*, the screens with crocodile-filled ponds prove quite difficult. It is possible to stand on the heads of the crocs only while their mouths are open, and a misstep lands Pitfall Harry in the water. As the player becomes more experienced, the player works up enough skill to jump quickly and deftly over the crocodiles, just like Heckle and Jeckle.

Jungle Generation

Part of the success of *Pitfall!* can certainly be attributed to its clean, clever amalgamation of popular culture icons. But the game's primary technical innovation is the size and complexity of the jungle environment.

Adventure boasted the first multiscreen graphical world in a game, an innovation that inspired *Pitfall!* and later action-adventure games. But *Adventure*'s castles and labyrinths were the same every time—they were hard-coded into the cartridge's ROM. Even in 1982, multiscreen VCS environments like the mansion in *Haunted House* or the caverns in *Raiders of the Lost Ark* were hand-designed and loaded from ROM. These environments may have seemed infinitely larger than the crude one-screen worlds of *Combat*, but they were small compared to the jungle in *Pitfall!* *Adventure* offered thirty different screens to explore. *Pitfall!* had 255.

Pitfall!, like *Adventure*, was burned on a 4K ROM. Crane's game required considerably more room just for storing graphics, though. Each of the sprites in *Pitfall!*—Harry, the cobra, the scorpion, the log, the crocodile, the various treasures, and so forth—have multiple animation frames, as well as color values for each display line. There is also data for the timer counter and the ubiquitous Activision logo at screen bottom. Yet the environment is considerably more detailed and expansive than that of *Adventure* in both total size and detail. Even accounting for the space used for Robinett's Easter egg, *Pitfall!* had to be highly compressed to fit in the same 4K that *Adventure* used.

Crane's solution to the puzzle of ROM mapping a large world with little ROM was to not store the world in ROM at all. Instead, the world is generated, consistently, by code.

Generated environments are common in games as far back as dungeon-crawlers like *Rogue*. But typically, after an environment is generated, it has to be stored in memory for use during play. For example, a new game of *SimCity* starts with a process of *terraforming*, in which the land, seas, mountains, forests, and rivers are created. In order for the player to be able to build a city atop it, the terrain data must then be saved somewhere, either on disk or in RAM. The Atari VCS has no disk storage, of course, and its paltry 128 bytes of RAM often provides barely enough room to manipulate the state of the game. (At any rate, even using all 128 bytes for storing the world would have provided only four bits of storage per screen in *Pitfall!*, which couldn't have sufficed.) There was not enough room in ROM or in RAM to store and manipulate the many screens of the *Pitfall!* jungle. Crane found another method of mapping this game's circular path, which was 255 screens in circumference.

The finished program uses an algorithm to generate each screen based on a screen definition. At the heart of this algorithm is a polynomial counter, a type of binary counter that increments in a pseudorandom sequence. Polynomial counters are frequently used in pseudorandom number generators; they work by counting in a specific but unusual order, for instance, (o, 6, 4, 6, 5, 3 . . .) instead of (o, 1, 2, 3, 4, 5, 6 . . .).

VCS programmers commonly used polynomial counters to create randomness in games—for example, to mix up the starting state of the pieces of the urn in *Haunted House*. But for the *Pitfall!* screens, Crane did not want random generation. Otherwise, the player would get a different screen if he moved Pitfall Harry off the left edge of a screen and then back again, making it impossible to mentally map the game world. For the screen definitions, Crane made a special counter that could be run either forward or backward. One version of the algorithm returned the next number in sequence; another returned the previous number. If Pitfall Harry runs off the right edge of the screen, the kernel uses the counter to get the next number in the sequence. If he runs back off the left edge, it gets the previous number.

On its own, an eight-bit number is still not adequate to render the many variations of an entire *Pitfall!* screen, which is composed of a particular jungle background (there are three different tree patterns, for variety), a scene pattern (holes, pits, crocodiles, and so on), the type of objects on the ground (logs, fire, treasure, and so on), and the position of the wall underground. The eight bits of each number in the counter sequence are used to define the settings for the screen:

bit 7: Underground pattern

bits 6–7: Tree patterns

bits 3–5: Ground pattern

bits 0–2: Object pattern

As stated here, the high bit of the scene description is actually used twice: once for the underground pattern (the location of the wall, if applicable), and once for the tree pattern, which needs two bits to count to three.

Because each number is guaranteed to remain consistent as the player moves back and forth through the world, each screen appears to be the same each time the player visits it. As every detail of the screen is based on that one number, the entire world can be computed algorithmically with very little memory. All told, the definition of the entire 255-screen jungle occupies less than 50 bytes of ROM.

Adventuring at Home

Because the Atari VCS offers so little processing time between frames, many cartridges use fixed patterns to define game levels. This is true for the wall patterns in *Combat*'s variations, the rooms in *Adventure*, the patterns of cars in *Grand Prix*, and many others. After time, players can begin to remember the patterns for these games and can greatly improve their performance. In one extreme example, David Crane described a marathon session of *Grand Prix* at the Consumer Electronics Show (CES) hospitality suite, in which he and others played all day trying to achieve the perfect game.[20]

But 255 screens of jungle adventure are much harder to memorize than are a couple minutes of auto racing. Before *Pitfall!*, most VCS game sessions were quite short. In the case of head-to-head games like *Combat* or *Boxing*, a session lasts only a few minutes. This is not surprising, given the fact that most early VCS cartridges were ports of arcade games, which offer short games so that players are compelled to drop another quarter in the coin slot.

Robinett's *Adventure* adapted the cave crawling text adventure, a genre with a play context very different from the tavern or arcade. The player of Crowther and Woods's *Adventure* would have sat at a terminal, probably in a nearly empty lab, where it would be possible to play for a while. Sessions of VCS adventure games like *Adventure* and *Superman* might not last much longer than arcade play would, though. *Adventure*'s easiest variant can be completed in less than two minutes, even by an inexperienced player.

Pitfall! offers a much longer game. A clock at the top of the screen counts down for twenty minutes. Before this time elapses, the player must find thirty-two treasures (eight each of money bag, gold bar, silver bar, diamond ring) within this time, while also avoiding logs and pits that reduce the score. Even when compared to Activision's previous games, *Pitfall!* was particularly well suited to the living room or den. In the arcade or the tavern, there is a social reason to limit gameplay, in addition to the financial incentive to increase coin-drop. But the living room invites people to consume media in much longer segments, such as the thirty-minute television show. The twenty-minute single-player session was an innovation, one that helped establish the experience of home console play. *Pitfall!* represents a moment when arcade play gave way to a different form of home console play.

The size and variation of the jungle contributes to the sophistication of *Pitfall!*, but so do other details in gameplay and presentation. Before *Pitfall!*, most VCS games offered one or two actions for the player—typically the options to move and shoot that can be seen in *Combat*. Even later, more visually striking titles like *Star Wars: The Empire Strikes Back* do essentially the same. The conventions of moving and shooting descend partly from arcade play, and they are certainly reinforced by the VCS controller, with its joystick and its single red button.

Pitfall! uses the same joystick controller, of course, with a button press making Pitfall Harry jump rather than fire. But in *Pitfall!*, moving and jumping allow several different modes of play, each requiring different skills. On one screen, the player has to run across an empty field, jumping over rolling logs. On the next, he must jump over holes to avoid falling underground. On another screen, he must jump and swing on a liana (a vine) over a pond, and on another, he must time his run to avoid waxing and waning quicksand, or to jump across crocodiles.

The game supports more than one action at different times, and sometimes demands more than one at about the same time—preparing to swing across a liana while avoiding rolling logs, for example. Taking the underground passages allows Pitfall Harry to move past three screens instead of one. Given the time constraints, it is impossible to collect all thirty-two treasures without using the passages, although using them subjects the player to the scorpion, and special care is required to vault over this opponent. As the *Pitfall!* manual summarizes, "You cannot excel at Pitfall! without acquiring a variety of skills." A variety of skills drawn from a very small number of possible actions (run, jump) characterizes the platformer genre, which *Pitfall!* helped establish. The Activision game built on previous arcade titles like *Donkey Kong* and looked ahead to side-scrolling, jumping adventures like *Super Mario Bros*.

The title also anticipated other, even later work. Although no one would call the game an "open-world game" in the style of *The Legend of Zelda* or *Grand Theft Auto*, there are gestures toward this type of experience in the way that *Pitfall!* builds on the graphical adventure conventions of Robinett's *Adventure*. *Pitfall!* features a large world that cannot be contemplated all at once. It offers a variety of actions built from a few core possibilities, each of which provides a unique experience and demands a different skill. And finally, it gives the player choices—even if limited ones—about where to go and what route to take to get there.

Attention to Detail

The *Pitfall!* jungle features multiple areas on each screen, making the game's kernel much more complex than earlier games, even though the overall program could not be larger. The routine that draws the screen closely matches Crane's original visualization of a setting for his little running man. Like many Activision games, *Pitfall!* creates a detailed on-screen image by splitting the screen up into horizontal sections. First the kernel draws the score and timer. Next come the trees and branches. Then it draws the top of the liana, then the liana and Pitfall Harry, then the ground, the pits, next the ladder and underground area, and finally the Activision logo and copyright.

Within each of these sections, Crane makes deft use of graphics drawing techniques that had become second nature by this time; namely, using the TIA graphics registers for visual elements different from their intended purposes and reusing those registers multiple times down the screen (see figure 6.2). For example, the leaves are drawn with a mirrored playfield, as are the tree trunks, but the more detailed branch segments where the trunks meet the leaves are rendered using sprite graphics, carefully positioned to match the location of the trunks and wide-doubled using the number-size registers. The liana is rendered with the ball graphic, which is moved slightly between each scan line to make it swing.

Those at Activision prided themselves on their richly colored, graphically sophisticated games, and players certainly noticed the difference. However, understanding the function of the TIA helps us appreciate the true attention to detail in a game like *Pitfall!* One such detail can be found in all Activision titles. Close inspection of the sides of a *Pitfall!* screen reveals a black bar at the left edge, but not at the right. The reason for this bar is partly aesthetic, partly technical.

To move a sprite, missile, or ball, the program must strobe the horizontal move (HMOVE) register after setting the horizontal position offset for the desired objects in their corresponding horizontal motion registers (HMP0/1, HMM0/1, HMBL). Once HMOVE is strobed (which is accomplished by writing any value to the register), the TIA executes the motion changes. However, to complete this process, the TIA requires that HMOVE

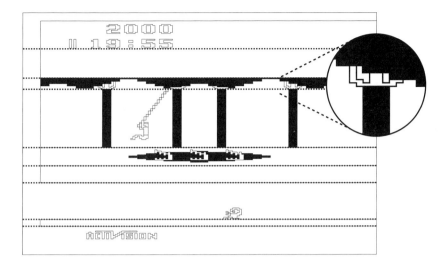

6.2 The distinct horizontal sections of a *Pitfall!* screen from the programmer's perspective. *Pitfall!* uses the TIA's graphics registers in ways that were not originally intended, as many games did around this time. In this image, areas drawn with playfield graphics are shaded in black. The branch details between the trunk and canopy are drawn with sprite graphics, as can be seen more easily in the inset detail.

take place immediately after a scan line synchronization (WSYNC), so that the TIA has enough time to update the horizontal locations of the objects before starting to draw the next line. As a result, doing additional processing between lines (which is almost always necessary) results in a short black bar on the left edge of the screen. In the photograph of the screen from *Star Wars: The Empire Strikes Back* (see jacket flap), black bars of this sort can be clearly seen.

The Activision designers thought this unintentional graphical effect was truly hideous, and they resolved never to have it appear in any of their games.[21] Because games like *Pitfall!* make liberal use of horizontal object motion in order to reuse different graphical elements for different purposes, it was necessary to strobe HMOVE. But to avoid an unsightly pattern of black bars, they strobed HMOVE on every line, ensuring that a black border would run continuously down the screen. In an emulator running on a modern computer, black bars caused by strobing HMOVE particularly stand out. CRT televisions of the early 1980s usually had casings that covered up the edges of the tube, however, so what was considered unsightly at Activision was even less noticeable, and the programming discipline at that company is even more remarkable.

Another graphical detail can be seen in the area where the liana attaches to the jungle canopy. There is a thin horizontal section of the screen at the bottom of the leaves where branches, liana, and leaves all need to be drawn on the same lines. The TIA offers only one register to set the color for both the playfield and the ball, so those two elements always render in the same color when drawn on the same scan line. For this reason, the top of the liana (drawn with the ball graphic) takes the green color of the leaves (drawn with playfield graphics). However, far from detracting from the credibility of the vine, the green-topped liana gives the impression of new growth at the jungle canopy. It doesn't seem to be an artifact of graphical sloppiness.

Activision's peer critique improved player experience, but it also could impose a considerable burden on programmers. By the time Crane had been persuaded to add additional lives to *Pitfall!*, the game was otherwise ready for release. He had already gone far beyond the 4K ROM limit, and back within it, many times, and had by his estimation spent "hundreds of hours" making the code smaller:

> Now I had to add a display to show your number of lives remaining, and I had to bring in a new character when a new life was used. The latter was easy. Pitfall Harry already knew how to fall, and how to stop when he hit the ground. So I dropped him from behind the tree cover down to the path. For the "Lives" indicator I added vertical tally marks to the timer display. That probably only cost 24 bytes, and with another 20 hours of "scrunching" the code I could fit that in.[22]

Creativity and Control

Two years after Activision's gang of four broke off from Atari, five other Atari programmers followed suit. Rob Fulop, Mark Bradley, Bill Grubb, Denis Koble, and Bob Smith teamed up with Jim Goldberger and Brian Dougherty from Mattel to found Imagic in 1981. By 1980, the programmers who were to found Imagic couldn't have been able to ignore Activision's early successes, which included *Dragster*, *Boxing*, *Fishing Derby*, and *Checkers*. Like Activision, Imagic established its own unique aesthetics, both in its games and its packaging. In addition to successful VCS titles like *Atlantis* and *Cosmic Ark*, Imagic started making its games for both the Atari VCS and the Intellivision, further distancing the concept of the third-party developer from any particular platform-making company. As the third-party marketplace grew, the studios made attempts not only

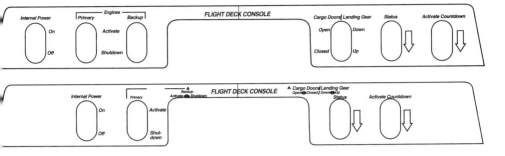

6.3   These paper overlays for *Space Shuttle* are intended to be placed on the Atari VCS console itself. They have cutouts for the VCS switches. Both of these overlays were provided with the cartridge so that the game could be played with either a six-switch console or a four-switch console. The creases in the center of the overlays are from where they were folded to fit in the box.

to differentiate their styles from those of Atari but also to differentiate them from one another.

One way that Activision addressed the VCS platform was by revisiting the different controllers available for it. Atari had shipped the console with both joystick and paddle controllers, but the latter quickly fell into disuse as arcade ports beyond *Pong* and *Breakout* became central to the system. The Activision cartridge *Kaboom!* made use of the paddle, allowing VCS owners to haul out this almost-forgotten controller.

Activision also experimented with more unusual ways to interact with the console. Steve Kitchen's *Space Shuttle: A Journey into Space* was a flight simulator for the spacecraft. The game used the joystick, and also used the console switches for gameplay rather than basic setup. The color/black-and-white and left difficulty switches became engine controls, the right difficulty became cargo door and landing gear levers, and the game select and reset switches were used for launch status controls. The game came with printed overlays (figure 6.3) to indicate these various functions.

Innovation in the use of VCS controllers certainly continued after the release of *Pitfall!*, as did the development of third-party games. Activision and Imagic were only the tip of the iceberg. And, with that metaphor in mind, it must be admitted that the enormous mass of third-party titles may have eventually played iceberg to the videogame industry's *Titanic*. In the months before the crash, though, Atari, Activision, Imagic, and others kept pushing the Atari VCS to do more, and the movies even claimed a beachhead in video gaming, occupying the silicon of Atari's leading home system.

Although it wasn't the first video game based on a movie,[1] the VCS *Star Wars: The Empire Strikes Back* does have the distinction of being the first video game of any sort that was based on any *Star Wars* movie. Standing at the beginning of this product line is quite notable, given that as of this writing there are about a hundred *Star Wars* video games—counting ports and contemporaneously developed versions of the same title for different platforms.

The toy company Parker Brothers found itself in an interesting place in the early 1980s, with a connection to *Star Wars* and an interest in the Atari VCS. Parker Brothers held the lucrative *Star Wars* licenses for toys and games. At this time, it still wasn't clear what home video games exactly were as products. Atari had an official opinion, which was expressed in a 1982 advertisement entitled "Everything You Always Wanted to Know About Atari Games, Etc, Etc.": "The ATARI Video Computer System™ Game is not a toy, to be put in the closet and forgotten. It's a permanent part of a home entertainment center." But Atari VCS games, like dedicated home systems before them, were shown at the International Toy Fair, sold at toy stores, and generally considered to be toys by the industry. The toy company Mattel even developed its own rival to the VCS—the Intellivision. So although the Atari VCS was often played by adults, and although the videogame industry was certainly recognized as a new force, it was still sensible for many reasons to consider the Atari VCS and cartridges for that system as toys. Parker Brothers certainly thought of VCS cartridges this way. The company claimed, based on this idea, that it had the exclusive right to develop *Star Wars* cartridges for the system.

As those at Parker Brothers contemplated how to exploit this valuable license, marketing manager Bill Bracy asked programmer Rex Bradford what could be done using the Atari VCS platform. What kinds of images could be created?

His comment was [that] actually it's possible to do fairly good graphics. I asked him to give me an example. A couple of days later he asked me to come into the programming area and take a look. There on the screen was a good representation of Darth [Vader]—his bust filled the screen. I seem to remember it had color and shading and looked far superior to anything I had seen in the games on the market at that time (fall of 1981). When I asked him what can we do with it, his response was: nothing! I've used up all the space.[2]

That single static display of an iconic *Star Wars* image, impressive as it was, filled the paltry standard amount of ROM (still 2K at the time) all by itself. It did turn out, however, that a *Star Wars* game—several games—could be coded for the Atari VCS. None that Parker Brothers would produce ended up including a detailed representation of a character's mask or face. That would be left for another movie-inspired game, *E.T.*, which featured a visage that peered out at the industry at the end of 1982 like a death's-head. The Parker Brothers games instead took a more abstract turn and played on the unique technologies and situations of the *Star Wars* universe.

Before explaining how *Star Wars: The Empire Strikes Back* works, how it was put together, and its specific relationship to the VCS platform, it is worthwhile to look at some cultural and economic factors that contributed to this game being contemplated in the first place. These have to do, first of all, with the involvement of the toy industry in video gaming, and, second, with the licensing of films and other properties for use in video games.

Bounced from the Toy Store

Long, long, ago, in an industry far, far away, Nolan Bushnell wanted to see if he could interest multiple retailers in selling his first product for the home, Atari's home *Pong* unit. He took the device to the International Toy Fair in New York, where he struck out completely—none of the companies there were willing to order even one. The device did end up getting distribution through Sears, the company that would also sell the Atari VCS as the Sears Telegames. At Sears, *Pong* landed not in the toy section but in the sporting goods department.

Although the toy industry didn't embrace video games, several toy companies did start making handheld electronic games with LED displays in the late 1970s.

Mattel, which sold Barbie and her friends, formed a subsidiary called Mattel Electronics and released its famous *Football* handheld in 1977; the next year saw the release of a new version that allowed passing. Several other sports followed, including *Baseball* and *Basketball*. Mattel Electronics went on to release the main rival to the Atari VCS, the Intellivision, in 1979.

In 1978 *Simon*, designed by television game pioneer Ralph Baer, hit the market. It was a game of imitation that itself imitated the Atari arcade game *Touch Me*, but expanded upon it by including colored buttons, improved sound, and of course a very different, smaller form factor. It was manufactured and sold by Milton Bradley, a company most famous for the board game *Life*, first published in 1860. In 1979, that company produced a remarkable innovation in handheld gaming: the first cartridge-based handheld. This was the Microvision, whose display had a mere 16 × 16 resolution. The system was engineered by Jay Smith. He went on to develop Milton Bradley's Vectrex, the first and only home vector-graphics console.

Merlin, with eleven buttons and six games, may or may not have been particularly wizardly. It was the top-selling system of the sort, though—king of the early handhelds. Shaped like a then-futuristic telephone (figure 7.1), the unit included tic-tac-toe, a *Simon*-like game, a *Mastermind*-like game, and the ability to use the unit as a musical instrument, which included recording and playback. It came from Parker Brothers.

There were games with electronic components that preceded these. An early one was Mattel's board game *Sonar Sub Hunt* from 1961. Other notable electronic games didn't arrive until the 1980s. These included the Nintendo Game and Watch systems and Coleco's two-player Head to Head sports games. But by the end of the 1970s, there was already a booming market for electronic games, ones that seemed more computer than toy. Companies were going beyond the electronic augmentation of board games into new form factors and game types.

Parker Brothers and other companies sold a billion dollars worth of handheld games in 1979, which didn't encourage them to look to the much smaller videogame market. In that market, the leading company, Atari,

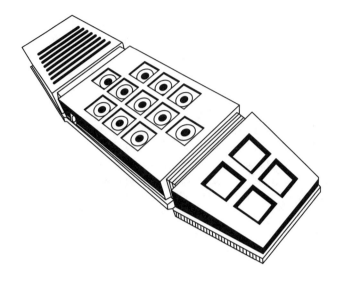

7.1 *Merlin*, from Parker Brothers, was the most popular of the handheld electronic games.

had sales of only $238 million during that same year—and that was after the Atari VCS had been on the market for more than twelve months. (Furthermore, the Atari figure overstates the home market by including the company's lucrative sales of arcade games.) Toy companies that were fixated on handhelds were jolted from their game in 1981, however, when the handheld gaming crash hit. By that time, the once-paltry home video-game market had grown to a respectable $1.2 billion, the Atari VCS was clearly a huge success, and Activision was a successful third-party publisher of VCS cartridges. Activision had even been joined by other VCS cartridge developers: Apollo and Imagic. The VCS cartridge market had been dismissed only two years before, but now seemed to be a land of opportunity.

So in 1981, Parker Brothers finally turned to the VCS and other home consoles. Its games would not reach shelves until 1982, the year that ended with the crash. Although the company was not experienced with videogame development, there were plans to create titles for several platforms. This, at least, made the company look better as a licensee than Atari would have. It must have been enough, anyway. No one managed to invalidate Parker Brothers' claim that its toy and game license included video games.

In U.S. toy industry reports and trade discussion, video games are implicitly and explicitly named as a threat to the "traditional toy industry" and revenues in these two categories are listed separately. Industry articles cheer reports about videogame violence, hoping that popular opposition will drive parents to spend more money on traditional toys. Yet toy companies continue to diversify into making video and electronic games and licensing their characters for use in video games. Today's "embrace and resist" approach to video gaming continues a complex history between toy companies and home video gaming.

License to Program

To recall the very beginning of the VCS era: when the system launched near the end of 1977, there were nine cartridges available from Atari. These were *Air-Sea Battle*, *Basic Math*, *Blackjack*, *Combat* (which was included with the system), *Indy 500*, *Star Ship*, *Street Racer*, *Surround*, and *Video Olympics*. Of these, at least five (*Air-Sea Battle*, *Combat*, *Star Ship*, *Surround*, and *Video Olympics*) were based to some extent on specific arcade games (*Anti-Aircraft*, *Tank*, *Starship 1*, *Blockade*, and *Pong*). Of the others, one was educational and one was a card game. The remaining two were racing games that also had arcade precedents, including games in the *Gran Trak* and *Sprint* series.

The first Parker Brothers catalog from 1982 also featured nine games, a selection that reflected how much the industry had changed in only a few years. The games listed—some of them still "coming soon" at this point—were *Amidar*, *Frogger*, *Reactor*, *Sky Skipper*, *Spider-Man*, *Star Wars: Jedi Arena*, *Star Wars: The Empire Strikes Back*, *Strawberry Shortcake Musical Matchups*, and *Super Cobra*. All of these nine were licensed games. Five were arcade ports that bore the same names as the corresponding coin-ops. One of the others was based on a comic book character, another drew on a greeting card character, and the remaining two were the *Star Wars* games. Although six of Atari's launch titles supported two-player simultaneous play, only one of the Parker Brothers games (*Star Wars: Jedi Arena*) let two people play at the same time. There was one educational, or "edutainment," title, *Strawberry Shortcake Musical Matchups*, which was advertised as "a fine first video game for little girls."

The first licensed game for the Atari VCS was *Superman*, programmed by John Dunn early in the history of the system, in 1978. Warner, the new owner of Atari, already owned the license rights to the Superman character. Although it's not exactly clear that the game is based on the movie,

Warner wanted to follow its *Superman* movie—rapidly—with a video game that was somehow tied to it. *Superman* was an innovative game, but not a big hit for Atari. This may have been part of the reason for the unusual dearth of licensed titles (other than coin-op conversions) until 1981. In the early 1980s, in a scramble that would more than make up for this lack, companies turned eagerly to licensing. Near the beginning of this period was the 1982 release of the movie *Tron*, the arcade game *Tron*, and several home console games based on the film, made by Mattel for the Atari VCS as well as the Intellivision.

Not only did the Atari VCS creators exploit movies and arcade games—they explored all sorts of curious characters and product tie-ins. Mattel went on to produce an Intellivision game and a entirely different VCS game based on a promotional character for a drink mix by General Foods. Both of these games were available by mail order and at retail stores and were called *Kool-Aid Man*. Other promotional games tied to particular retail products included *Chase the Chuckwagon* and *Tooth Protectors*, which were available only to those who mailed in proof of purchase stamps. Atari made an agreement with the Children's Television Workshop to produce four Sesame Street titles that would work with a special oversized keypad controller for kids. And Data Age published a VCS game to promote a popular band: *Journey Escape*.

It's hard to finger any aspect of the Atari VCS platform that may have hastened or slowed the growth of licensed titles. The representational power of the machine was slight in comparison to today's consoles with their 3D graphics and full-motion video, but there were manuals and box materials to create the necessary associations. Anyway, a lack of representational power never prevented properties from being licensed for other non-electronic game forms and for various toys. When the question was whether to license a property for use in a video game, the answer always was based on corporate concerns, not technical or creative factors. The precedent of the conversion of arcade games was important. Converting its own games gave Atari the idea that another company's game, such as Taito's *Space Invaders*, could be licensed and converted. There was also Atari's acquisition by media giant Warner Communications, which in the short term, surprisingly, led only to the development of *Superman*. The later licensing of *E.T.* for use in a video game was an initiative from Warner, not from within Atari: Warner's CEO Scott Ross secured the *E.T.* license after extensive negotiations, while Atari's head, Ray Kassar, called the *E.T.* game "a dumb idea."[3] Beyond this, the particular influence of the 1977 *Star Wars* as a transmedial story that manifested itself in action figures, die-cast space ships, and many other sorts of lucrative forms off the screen cannot be ignored.

Attack of the Movie-Game

The first video game based on a movie or television series is probably Mike Mayfield's 1971 text-only game *Star Trek*, a strategy game about commanding the USS *Enterprise* against the Klingons. But Mayfield created the game as a hobbyist on a Sigma 7 minicomputer, a device that required as much space as several refrigerators. It hardly seemed to be at risk of becoming a commercial product.

The first commercial video game based on a movie seems to be Atari's own *Shark Jaws*, released just after Steven Spielberg's popular film *Jaws* in 1975. *Shark Jaws* was not an officially licensed product. Reportedly, Atari tried to acquire the license, failed to do so, and decided to make the game anyway. The Atari game's name might sound reasonably different from the title of the Spielberg film, but the cabinet art used a typeface that mimicked the one in *Jaws* marketing materials, and "Shark" was printed on the cabinet in tiny letters next to the enormous word "Jaws" (figure 7.2) Aware of the riskiness of this unofficial game, Bushnell, ever the daredevil, created a new company called Horror Games to shelter Atari from litigation. The game itself was simple, built as a modification of the *Tank* circuitry. The player steered a diver trying to catch a fish while avoiding a shark.

Shark Jaws was followed by Exidy's controversial *Death Race*, developed by Howell Ivey. This was the first video game to encourage simulated automotive homicide. Players were challenged to kill highly abstract humanoid figures ("gremlins," according to the instructions) with their vehicles. The game's rollout occasioned a media frenzy. *Death Race* was denounced on *60 Minutes* and featured in *The National Enquirer*. This did wonders for sales of the cabinet, for a short time, but before long the protests led Exidy to capitulate and pull the game from the market. The 1976 *Death Race* was clearly an attempt to play upon the success of the 1975 movie *Death Race 2000*, an offering from the privileged, refined media channel of the cinema that was produced by Roger Corman and starred David Carradine and Sylvester Stallone. Exidy also did not negotiate a license for the movie that its game riffed on. Exidy and Atari were not alone in taking this course. In 1980 EduWare took the risk of releasing an unlicensed Apple][game called *The Prisoner* that was clearly based on the British television series of the same name.

7.2 Advertising and cabinet art from the one-sheet for *Shark Jaws*, with one of the two words of the title much more strongly emphasized. The title of the film *Jaws*, as it was typeset in promotional posters, is inset in the bottom left.

Because the Atari VCS was already being fed by arcade ports, it wasn't too much of a stretch for those at Atari to consider whether the movies might also supply them with material. It was even less of a stretch for media company Warner Communication, owners of Atari since 1976.

Howard Scott Warshaw's *Raiders of the Lost Ark* is an innovative adventure game that transforms a movie into something playable on the Atari VCS. It is in the same vein as Robinett's *Adventure*, but much more intricate and graphically advanced. Particular scenes and settings from the movie are fairly clearly represented in the *Raiders* cartridge, which features a splash screen, a diverse world, numerous graphically detailed objects, an unusual control scheme in which one player used both joysticks, and in-game music. The cartridge may have made the most significant advances in the action-adventure genre between the appearance of Robinett's *Adventure* in 1978 and the debut of *The Legend of Zelda* for the NES in Japan in 1985. *Raiders* added a graphical inventory and subquests, helping to focus and refine the action-adventure genre. The cartridge ended up being a hit for Atari. It helped land Warshaw another Spielberg project, one with a seemingly impossible deadline.

That project was *E.T.: The Extra-Terrestrial*, which Warshaw managed to complete in only five weeks. (In comparison, Warshaw said he put in four or five months of work on *Yars' Revenge* and six or seven months on *Raiders*.) The ill-fated 1982 film-licensed game followed in the tradition of *Adventure*, *Superman*, and *Raiders*, using between-screen navigation and challenging the player to avoid colliding with scientists and police. *E.T.* has been ranked, more than once, as the worst video game of all time. Atari's financial collapse is sometimes attributed to this one specific game—although this is certainly an exaggeration. A legend tells of mounds of unsold *E.T.* cartridges being buried by Atari in the New Mexico desert.[4] The legend is likely true, too. Although *E.T.* was not specifically named, the *New York Times* did report that fourteen truckloads of equipment, including game cartridges, were dumped at an Alamogordo landfill and covered in concrete while guards kept reporters and other would-be spectators away from the site.[5]

There are certainly reasons for the poor quality of *E.T.* Most obviously, the development schedule—imposed because of the pending holiday shopping season—precluded a high-quality game, unless one were to be developed by some incredible stroke of luck. A general problem that the makers of licensed games faced was the need to tailor their schedules to the release of other media properties or to the Christmas season, along with the need to maintain qualities of the particular property being used. All of this was added to the usual constraints and pressures provided by the platform and the market. Conceptually, regardless of the production pressure that was brought on by the Christmas deadline, *E.T.* suffered from the potential inappropriateness of translating a film largely about the relationship between a boy and a helpless alien into a work focused on moving around and running into things.

Although the arcade may have been the first to host an exploitation film game (*Death Race*), at least one third-party developer for the Atari VCS wanted to see if it could out-schlock the coin-ops. Wizard Video

Games acquired the licenses to *The Texas Chainsaw Massacre* and *Hallow-een*, releasing both of these oddities in 1983. *The Texas Chainsaw Massacre* allows the player to control the villain Leatherface and run around chain-sawing victims, bloodlessly and pointlessly. This is not a typical move in modern-day horror games, but perhaps, along with *Death Race*, it is one of the early works that anticipates the crime-spree possibilities of the *Grand Theft Auto* series. Ed Salvo, who programmed for the then-defunct company Apollo and ended up forming a company called VSS, took on the job of programming *The Texas Chainsaw Massacre* for Wizard, completing it in about six weeks. *Halloween*, which lets the player control the innocent "last girl" and which features beheadings with spurting blood, had been handed off to another programmer at VSS. By the time these two games hit the market, the Atari VCS had suffered a chain store massacre and the titles, even though they were designed for controversy, didn't manage to create much of a stir.

Imperial Technology

Parker Brothers ended up using the *Star Wars* name and properties in four VCS titles: *Star Wars: The Empire Strikes Back*, *Star Wars: Jedi Arena*, *Star Wars: Death Star Battle*, and *Star Wars: The Arcade Game*. Another game, *Star Wars: Ewok Adventure*, was developed but never released. *Star Wars: The Empire Strikes Back* was the first to market and was the lead title in Parker Brothers' first catalog of Atari VCS cartridges, coming right before the famous *Frogger*. This first *Star Wars* game was later ported to the Intellivision and Atari 5200.[6] All versions of *Star Wars: The Empire Strikes Back* featured very similar gameplay and graphics, although there are telltale signs of the different platforms.

Bill Bracy described the process of developing the concept for this game and its basic gameplay: "A small group of us, including traditional game designers, video game players, and a couple of us in marketing brainstormed on the various scenes from *The Empire Strikes Back* and started developing storyboards and experimenting with game techniques. We prioritized the game elements we wanted to include and watched the list diminish as the available cartridge space was used up."[7]

Although the game was still programmed by an individual (Bradford, in this case, working with designer Sam Kjellman) in a way that was typical of VCS development, this development process was unlike Atari's. At Atari, a programmer was essentially shut in a room alone for a few months and left to develop a game. Often, the VCS programmer took an existing arcade game that would be the basis for the cartridge. But when an "original" concept needed to be devised at Atari in the heyday of VCS programming, from 1977 through 1983, it would be the work of a programmer, not a task force.

Although many elements may have dropped off the wish list that Parker Brothers' team developed, *Star Wars: The Empire Strikes Back* built upon five years of VCS development to include features that would have made jaws drop at Atari back in 1977. And it was devised by a programmer who not only was working at a different company—he had *never* worked at Atari. How did this programmer, Rex Bradford, learn to develop VCS games? He explained: "Our first job was to reverse-engineer the trade-secret Atari [VCS]. Parker Brothers hired a company to strip off the top of the graphics chip and photograph it. [Two engineers] stared at the circuit diagram, while I wrote a disassembler to examine existing cartridge code. Then I started writing some small programs to test our theories about how it worked. Finally, by the fall of 1981, we were ready to create our first game."[8]

In some ways, the first game that Bradford completed resembles Eugene Jarvis's 1980 arcade game *Defender*, which was ported to the Atari VCS in 1981 by Bob Polaro. *Star Wars: The Empire Strikes Back* is also a smoothly side-scrolling shooter in which the player's small ship, the snowspeeder, can move left or right along terrain, wrapping around the playing field (figure 7.3) as can be done in *Defender*. The same type of long-range view of opponents that this earlier game offers is also present in *Star Wars: The Empire Strikes Back*. But beyond that, there are significant differences. There are no people running around on the ground who need to be defended from abduction. Whereas *Defender* has a host of different enemies who behave very differently, Bradford's game has only the massive Imperial walkers. These can fire two types of weapons, one ballistic and one "smart." Both types of enemy fire can be shot down by the snowspeeder. The snowspeeder can also land and a limited number of repairs can be undertaken. The level of damage to the snowspeeder and to walkers is indicated by their color, which shifts through green and red into yellow.

The Imperial walkers are visually and formally formidable. They are drawn in a rather elaborate way. A sprite scaled at 4× is used for the body of a walker, in the top half of the screen. Then, a sprite scaled 2× is situated directly below to provide the legs. Both are effectively eight "pixels" wide, although the sizes of these two pixels are not the same, so that the top half appears twice as blocky as the legs. This technique makes it easy to make the body "solid," while the legs are not. The effect is an opponent whose Imperial scale dwarfs the Rebel snowspeeder, effectively evoking

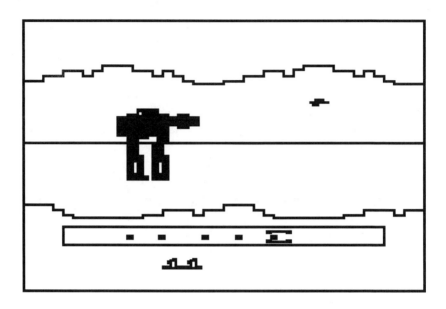

7.3 The tiny, agile snowspeeder, which the player controls, faces—or in this case, runs away from—one of an endless supply of huge Imperial walkers.

the snowspeeder sequence in the film but also resonating with the *Star Wars* Death Star infiltration and battle, the opening sequence of the original film in which a giant Imperial craft overwhelms a Rebel ship, and the overall *Star Wars* mythos of an agile, individual, human-scale resistance to a lumbering, enormous tyranny. It is not just the large visual scale of the walkers that gives this sense—they are also extremely difficult to destroy, requiring forty-eight shots, unless the player uses one of the other two methods to dispatch them: firing into a bomb hatch or, less sustainably, crashing the snowspeeder against the walker's body in one of the variants where the walkers are solid.

The cartridge didn't have the "bosses" that would come to typify shooters, ending each of the levels and presenting a culminating, massive challenge to the player. The boss had only recently been introduced in the 1980 arcade game *Phoenix* in the form of the mothership. Nevertheless, in *Star Wars: The Empire Strikes Backs* the standard opponents, the Imperial walkers, seem boss-like in many ways. They are huge compared to the player's craft and they take many, many shots to kill. They also feature an intermittently appearing "weak point," something that could be seen in *Phoenix* but which in later games often was taken as a cue from *Star Wars: The Empire Strikes Back*. In the game, a blinking "bomb hatch" appears at random in one of a few locations on the Imperial walkers, remaining for only a short time. If the snowspeeder fires into it, the enemy can be dispatched in a single shot.

Another clever touch gave some 3D sense to the game. As the snowspeeder is moved to the edges of the screen, the line defining the mountains in the background moves left and right at half the rate that the icy crags in the foreground move. This technique, commonly called "parallax scrolling," also works to make the game more exhilarating and to increase the feeling of velocity that sets the player's snowspeeder apart from the mighty but slow Imperial walkers.

Despite these interesting features, Bradford has looked back modestly at his first effort for the Atari VCS, created without any official information on programming the platform, as being "not that technically advanced" for a VCS cartridge.[9] The design and programming process at Parker Brothers worked well, though, and the result got *Star Wars* off to a good start in the videogame arena.

The Players Are Listening

One of the unusual features of the first *Star Wars* game is its use of a short but recognizable tune that plays as introductory and in-game music. Although continual sound effects were common in VCS games, it is hard to produce anything that sounds like Western music on the machine. The frequencies that the TIA can generate miss most of the chromatic scale. When Garry Kitchen was working as a programmer for Activision, he went through and marked the notes that the Atari VCS could hit. He then asked a professional composer of jingles to put something together using only those notes. The impressive composition that resulted from this constrained process can be heard at the beginning of *Pressure Cooker*. Parker Brothers managed to do pretty well with introductory musical numbers, too, as it demonstrated in its first release, *Frogger*, which mimics the music of the arcade game. *Raiders of the Lost Ark* also features a opening theme that recalls that of the movie.

It was not simple to produce melodious music, though. Programmers at Atari would often not attempt to do so, treating the TIA like a percussion instrument instead and creating musical sounds through rhythm.[10] The distinctive monotone sound at the end of a *Missile Command* level provides an example of the effective use of this technique. James Andreasen's 1982 *Haunted House* integrated percussive sounds (of footsteps) with short in-game "tunes" indicating the ascent or descent of a stairway and other sound effects. The game, which was also among the first to use player-controlled scrolling between portions of a large virtual space, made up for its rather underwhelming graphics with effective sound design.

Playing a tune during gameplay, rather than in an introductory sequence or at a point where play is paused, introduces additional difficulties. It has to be accomplished in the vertical blanking interval along with the main game logic. This can be done, as modern-day VCS programmer Paul Slocum showed when he hacked *Combat* to create the 2002 cartridge *Combat Rock*. His modified game looks and functions exactly like the original, but the sound effects have been replaced with a recognizable version of "Rock the Casbah" by the Clash that plays continually. Still, playing music during a game is hardly straightforward.

When the snowspeeder endures for two minutes in *Star Wars: The Empire Strikes Back*, it wins the temporary invulnerability of "the Force" and the *Star Wars* theme plays, as it does when the cartridge first starts up. This rare musical treat effectively draws a connection to the *Star Wars* movies and also works effectively in the game, making the period of invulnerability even more heightened. The theme plays as sound effects from the game continue, too, so that it is integrated into the experience of play rather than interrupting it.

Bradford also made great use of the 128-color VCS palette, cycling the defeated walkers through a luminous magenta and neighboring colors. When the walkers advance all the way across the screen to inevitably defeat the player, the sky color-cycles in the same manner. The Atari VCS *Star Wars: The Empire Strikes Back* plays on a strength of the system: unlike the sixteen-color Intellivision, the Atari VCS supplies numerous colors suitable for use in skies and sunsets. The colors of the Atari VCS had already been used to display a beautiful sunset, in fact, in an Activision game released the previous year: Steve Cartwright's *Barnstorming*. The landscape painter for that game wasn't Cartwright, though. He had lifted the sunset code and data from a program called "the Venetian blinds demo," a simulation of a window written by Activision's David Crane. Other Activision sunsets appeared in *Chopper Command*, *Seaquest*, and *Frostbite*.

Although the VCS palette for NTSC graphics includes the saturated colors that became emblematic of Activision as well as colors that worked well to fill the sky, the options didn't suit every visual purpose. Flesh tones were pretty much missing, making portraits of E.T. and Darth Vader easier to manage than images that looked like ordinary faces. One reaction to this was to ignore this limitation and paint the character's skin some shade of pink or yellow. This was the route taken by the company Mystique, which produced so-called pornographic cartridges for the Atari

VCS, including *Bachelor Party*, *Beat 'Em and Eat 'Em*, and the particularly odious *Custer's Revenge*. (In that game, the player directs a naked man to traverse a battlefield and enact the rape—or consensual rape-fantasy penetration, if you have a liberal interpretation of the game and the manual—of a Native American woman tied to a post.) But other developers chose scenarios and scenes so that they could use color effectively (and more tastefully). This sometimes allowed dramatic effects to be displayed to viewers who, plugging in a joystick, found the television above the port to be the color of sky.

The Sun Sets on Atari's Empire

The scenario of *Star Wars: The Empire Strikes Back* is similar to that of *Space Invaders* and many other arcade games, in that the enemy continually keeps coming. There is no way to win—only the possibility of holding out for a longer or shorter period of time. The interesting thing about this game structure is that it is perfectly consistent with the corresponding sequence from the movie *The Empire Strikes Back*, in which the Rebel Alliance is unable to repulse an attack on its Hoth base by Imperial walkers and can hope only to hold them off for a while.

As has already been mentioned, upstart Atari and all the makers of VCS games found themselves in the situation of the Rebel Alliance by 1983. The causes of the crash were several. Many game players were looking to home computers rather than videogame consoles by this point. A variety of interesting computer games were available, and there were reasons to prefer home computers. They could be used for word processing, programming, and telecommunications as well. It didn't hurt, from the user's perspective, that whereas cartridges were extremely difficult to duplicate, computer games could be typed in from listings in magazines or, if they were on cassette or floppy disk, easily duplicated and shared.

While the popularity of home computers was growing, a flood of VCS games entered the marketplace in 1982 and posed a problem for the industry. Orders from retailers were overambitious, and cartridges ended up returned or deeply discounted in the bargain bin. Feeling burned, many retailers chose not to place new orders. There were so many titles that consumers had a hard time discerning which ones were likely to be enjoyable and which were likely to turn into clearance cartridges that were a fifth the price of newly released titles—perhaps worth even less than this. The first wave of returns and the ensuing sales slump forced most of the third-party developers out of business. *E.T.* almost certainly does not bear sole responsibility for the crash, but, like a finger pointing to the moon, it shows that the industry was putting effort into licensing rather than design and programming, inundating the market with less innovative work that had been forced through the development process quickly.

This crash was not the end of the Atari VCS—or, as it had come to be known by this time, the Atari 2600. But it was the end of one incarnation of Atari, a company that had already been transformed under Warner, and it was the end of the boom years for the first popular cartridge-based system. Many thought that it was end of video games, which they imagined were a passing fad. This line of thinking wasn't correct or productive, but it did allow the American videogame industry to be greatly outpaced by Japan's Nintendo and Sega, companies that continued to innovate with the next generation of consoles, the Famicom (Nintendo Entertainment System) and SG-1000 Mark III (Sega Master System). In the context of the toy industry's troubled relationship with video gaming, and given how the industry was burned by the crash, Nintendo managed to persuade American retailers to stock its system only by packaging it with a robot and a light gun so that it became recognizable as a toy.

Nintendo also learned from Atari's harsh lesson. When Atari designed and released the Atari VCS in the mid-1970s, it seems unlikely that anyone at the company seriously imagined that games could be made for it by some other entity. When many other companies did exactly that, Atari had no way to control which titles appeared on its system. Nintendo devised a way to support retailers and third-party developers—yet also to control them. The company's first-party licensing method required outside developers to submit applications to qualify for third-party status, to buy official development kits from Nintendo, and to submit their titles for review, quality assurance, and release planning. Nintendo used the system both to police quality and to limit the number of games that each developer could produce per year, preventing another glut of titles. Nintendo convinced retailers that games bearing its quality seal would sell well, and this method worked.

Without Nintendo's leap, the retail videogame marketplace might not have recovered from the 1983 downturn—at least, not as quickly as it did. But video games paid a price for their renewed commercial success. Activision had thrived thanks to strong creative vision and experimentation. Nintendo's first-party licensing model set the stage for the more homogeneous and anonymous work-for-hire mode of videogame development that remains the norm. It also introduced a culture of "soft censorship" in video games, with console manufacturers getting the last word on what they would and wouldn't allow on their hardware.

Things could have come about very differently. Noting Atari's success and name recognition in North America and worldwide, in 1983 Nintendo asked Atari to bring the Famicom Computer System (what would become the NES in North America) to market outside Japan. Before a deal could be struck, Atari CEO Ray Kassar was forced out of the company over allegations of insider trading.[11] Chaos struck Atari upper management, and Nintendo eventually lost patience and released the NES on its own. A combination of pride and humility can be seen in Atari's reaction to Nintendo's console, which numerous executives witnessed firsthand during a trip to Kyoto. In a memo circulated mid-1983 about the deal, Atari executive Don Teiser compares the prototype NES to MARIA, the code name for the Atari 7800 that was currently in development at Atari. "It appears to be a superior machine," writes Teiser, "but the MARIA chip is not yet finished."[12]

Despite internal turmoil at the company, Atari's console remained important in the mid-1980s as the next generation of video gaming was rolled out. Along technological and business dimensions, Nintendo's system was among the platforms most directly influenced by the Atari VCS. Atari's system has remained influential both as a distant technological ancestor of today's home consoles and as a residual but compelling presence in today's gaming landscape.

The Atari VCS had one of the longest production runs of any microcomputer, and certainly the longest of any dedicated home videogame console. Models were manufactured from 1977 through 1992. Commercial games continued to be released after the crash of 1983, with many appearing for the first time as late as 1987. That year, for example, Atari released *Realsports Boxing*, a side-view boxing game with realistic boxers, a ring, and spectators that far outdid the once-spectacular *Boxing* cartridge by Bob Whitehead, released by Activision way back in 1980.

Lower-cost electronics contributed to such advances. *Realsports Boxing* uses à 16K ROM, allowing eight times as much code and data as the original cartridges did. But new conventions for gameplay also began to feed back into VCS game design. Just as games like *Adventure* and *Pitfall!* set conventions and expectations for future games, so the next generation of titles introduced new design challenges on the VCS platform. By 1987, Nintendo and Sega's eight-bit systems had been on the market for two full years in the United States and longer in Japan. The VCS titles from the late 1980s often adapted the conventions of games produced for such newer home consoles, also borrowing from contemporary arcade games that were unimaginable ten years earlier. For example, *Realsports Boxing* includes a character selection screen; players choose to play as boxers with unique styles and names like Iron Fists and Lefty O'Leary. Instead of a single punch verb enacted by the joystick button, *Realsports Boxing* accepts more complex combinations of button and directional input, translating these into different moves: hook, jab, or uppercut. Systems like the NES, which had two action buttons compared to the Atari VCS's one, and ever more complex arcade machines, which often sported handfuls of different buttons, had made more elaborate inputs common.

The Atari VCS had begun as a home console for ports of popular coin-op games, mainly *Pong* and *Tank*; within a few years, it hosted *Space Invaders*, *Pac-Man*, and games that were inspired by coin-ops, including *Yars' Revenge*. Later, the machine became a platform for adaptations of popular movies—the *Star Wars* films, *E.T.: The Extra-Terrestrial*, and even *Porky's*. A decade after the system launched, ports remained a strong influence, but in some cases the games being ported were ones that themselves followed conventions established earlier on the Atari VCS.

That it was possible to complete a game like *Realsports Boxing*—even on a 16K ROM—testifies to the flexibility of the Atari VCS's architecture. The abstract simplicity of the machine, combined with the stringent constraints that simplicity imposed, made for an extremely flexible system. A more rigid hardware design, such as that found in consoles of the late 1990s and early 2000s, with their support for real-time 3D graphics, can provide for more sophisticated visual presentations, but such a design also reduces the breadth of representations that are possible. The minimal design of the Atari VCS actually maximized what could be done with its small amount of computation, making it a more versatile platform for creative expression that it would have been with, for instance, built-in sprites and hardware facilities that were well-adapted to drawing 2D, overhead-view playfields, but were not adaptable to any other perspective.

This simplicity continued to invite new innovations well into the late 1980s. In 1987, Exus released a new VCS controller, the first since the *Track & Field* controller of 1984.[1] The controller was a pressure-sensitive mat that rested on the floor in front of the television, emblazoned with five different-colored circles. Depressing any of these with a foot or hand had the effect of closing a joystick switch or pressing the red button, inputs for which designer could program appropriate responses. The device was called the "Foot Craz" (figure 8.1). Two games were bundled with it, *Video Jogger* and *Video Reflex*. *Video Jogger* is a simple running game similar to the running events in *Track & Field*. But rather than depress buttons rapidly, the player has to run—literally—on the sensors of the Foot Craz. *Video Reflex* was a Whack-a-Mole-style game played with the feet. On-screen, bugs appear in one of five colored regions. The player has a limited time to depress the sensor corresponding to the correct colored region.

Foot Craz preceded Bandai's Family Fun and Fitness, which Nintendo licensed in 1988 and released as the Power Pad. It took more than a decade

8.1   This first mat controller, by Exus, entered the market too late to enjoy commercial success. The layout of the controller differs considerably from that of both the Nintendo Power Pad and later *Dance Dance Revolution* mats.

for this type of controller to achieve widespread popularity in the home, but it finally did when Konami adapted its popular arcade dancing game *Dance Dance Revolution* for the Dreamcast and PlayStation. Since then, publishers, players, and even HMOs and municipal governments have become interested in the ways that input devices for video games can encourage physical activity. Yet this idea was first explored on the humble Atari VCS in the tenth year of that console's life.

Playing On

Even though the Atari VCS continued to be manufactured in small quantities into the early 1990s, its commercial viability was exhausted by the late 1980s. Exus's Foot Craz—the only product that company ever made—

enjoyed so little success in the market that the mat and its games are among the rarest VCS collectibles.

Among the rarest, yes—but certainly not the only collectible items. The Atari VCS has been a great platform for collectors and is clearly the centerpiece of collectors' gatherings such as the Classic Gaming Expo, even though other platforms are well represented. Original systems of different models, from the first wood-grained, six-switches-on-the-front "heavy sixer" to the smaller, black 2600 Jr., remain widely available from specialty stores and by online auction. Plenty of famous cartridges are easy to acquire, while a wide range of arcana is available to those who want to pursue cartridges more earnestly and are willing to spend more money. In addition to offering collectors a low threshold and a high ceiling, VCS cartridges are fairly durable, as are the consoles themselves, so it is possible for collectors to play games from their hoard as well as admiring them.

Just as Atari wanted to provide a way for families to play their favorite coin-op games at home in the late 1970s and early 1980s, the recent owners of Atari's intellectual property and brand have sought to give Xbox and PlayStation players an opportunity to access their favorite Atari VCS games on their current home consoles. The *Atari Anthology*, released in 2004, collects dozens of VCS and arcade games along with additional documentation, art, and resources from the creation and marketing of the original titles.

Rereleases of VCS games on new consoles pose special challenges. Getting older games to run on newer systems requires either writing an emulator to implement the Atari VCS in software or simply rewriting each game entirely, recreating each one on the new platform. Either method introduces problems. Even an ideal emulator cannot provide an Xbox with the original controls, such as difficulty switches that can be easily toggled by either player during a game, or other affordances of the original hardware. Differences in display technology on modern monitors make emulated VCS games look different than they did on a late 1970s or early 1980s television. But recreating games from scratch is even harder, and requires extensive effort for each game being redone. As we have tried to show in this book, the material constraints of the VCS hardware can be seen as providing opportunities for the creative process—not obstacles. The increased power of modern computers, and their different set of limitations, can sometimes make it very difficult to accurately port games.

The Stella emulator is free software that works on Windows, Mac OS X, and Linux, and that essentially implements the Atari VCS in software.

It gives computer users the ability to play VCS games, once the ROM images for those games have been acquired. (These are files that are generally 2K, 4K, or 8K in size and that contain all the data that was stored in the original cartridges.) Downloading Stella does not provide the user with authentic controllers, of course, or supply one's computer with a wood-grain finish.

A commercial emulator is provided in the *Atari Anthology*, which collects many coin-op games along with its VCS titles.[2] Among these are the arcade game *Asteroids*. Modern plasma and LCD high-definition televisions (HDTVs) have no electron beam and thus are not capable of drawing a picture in the same way as it would have been seen on an early VCS display—and certainly not on the XY graphics display of a game such as *Asteroids*. However, they can display pictures at very high resolution. The *Atari Anthology* port was able to capture some of the high-resolution nature of *Asteroids* by converting it to HD. As of this writing, *Atari Anthology* is the only title for the original Xbox that supports 1080i HD resolution.

The toy company Jakks Pacific has produced a "television game" joystick and a set of paddles that plug directly into a TV and contain a selection of games. The Jakks units recreate the physical interfaces to the Atari VCS, which the *Atari Anthology* does not do, but they offer reimplemented rather than emulated games.

A good combination of controllers and authentic game function is provided in Atari's Flashback 2, released in 2005 with forty built-in games and two detachable joysticks. This is the most recent hardware implementation of the Atari VCS to be mass-manufactured. The system was designed by Curt Vendel, who also runs the Atari History Museum. It lacks a cartridge port, although it is possible (if not extremely practical) to undertake a hardware modification and add one. The Flashback 2 mimics the appearance of the first model of the Atari VCS and includes a faithful implementation of the original VCS board, all on a single low-cost chip.

Another way that VCS games live on is through lower-powered, lower-resolution devices. In the recent past this has meant platforms such as the Nintendo Game Boy Color; today, the more desirable targets are mobile phones. The outcomes of cell phone ports are usually poor. Incompatible interfaces are one reason—users control mobile devices differently than arcade cabinets or home consoles. But the difference in graphics systems is an even more severe problem.

The element of the Atari VCS that stands out when the system is held up to other platforms is the TIA. Even if the machine had been built with a different processor, or had been shipped with controls of some different design, the constraints of the TIA—two sound channels, the line-by-line rendering requirements, the sprite-missile-ball graphics, and so forth—would have left this hypothetical, modified Atari VCS with a similar look and feel when it comes to programming and play. The TIA is strongly tied to the nature of the television's CRT display. In the context of the home console experience of 1977–1983, that the system was "video" was about as important as that it was "computer." The Atari VCS is certainly not just a "video" device in the generic sense of being able to display a moving image: its TIA was designed to interface with a particular type of video and audio hardware, a television set. All of its unique features emanate from this.

Perhaps because of the special nature of the TIA, or perhaps because of the limitless human capacity for technical fascination, programmers have continued to hack at and develop original VCS games. There is a thriving hobbyist community that has picked up the Atari VCS, using and refining emulators, writing disassemblers and development tools, and even manufacturing cartridges and selling them, complete with boxes and manuals. This "homebrew" scene could be seen, strictly speaking, as continuing the commercial life of the Atari VCS, but the community is not very corporate. It operates on the scale of zines and unsigned bands, with most recent ROMs offered for free online—even if they are also sold in limited releases of a few hundred copies in cartridge form.

Although many homebrew programmers are motivated by nostalgia, they are doing more than recreating the glory days of the Atari VCS—they are continuing to discover previously unknown capabilities of the platform. Paul Slocum, who has completed *Combat Rock*, *Synthcart*, and impressive work toward a Homestar Runner game, managed to add a system for background music. Andrew Davie, who did the PAL game *Qb*, devised a way of alternating colors on different frames to achieve the visual effect of more than 128 colors. Thomas Jentzsch, creator of *Jammed* and *Thrust*, devised a new bidirectional scrolling technique and, working with Fabrizio Zavagli, also converted a slew of VCS games between NTSC and PAL. The list of recent technical achievements and recent original games goes on and on.

The Atari VCS has found uses in other domains, blasting into the space of the museum and the worlds of art and music. Yucef Merhi first exhibited a piece including an Atari VCS, *net@ari*, in 1985, and has created a series of *Atari Poetry* works that run on the platform since then—*Atari Poetry* I through *IV*, initially; then, in 2005, *Super Atari Poetry*; *Atari Poethree* in 2006; and, most recently, in 2007, *atari ex machina*. Slocum's band TreeWave and several other musicians have used *Synthcart* as a part of live music performances. In 2006, Mary Flanagan first exhibited her nine-foot-tall *[giant]oystick]*, a scaled-up but fully functional controller for the Atari VCS, modeled after the original joystick for the system.

Atari's venerable system has also been used to help students learn and engage with the history of creative computing. In 2005, the twenty-four-hour Retro Redux event at New York University challenged students in the area to design Atari VCS games. Both of the authors of this book have had students play and analyze games on the system; Ian Bogost has also had them program their own original games in Batari BASIC and assembly.[3]

The influence of the Atari VCS continues to be recognized by gamers, designers, those involved with computing, and the world at large. Numerous lists of top games throughout history are studded with VCS titles. The founders of Activision were given the Game Developer's Choice First Penguin Award in 2003 for founding the first third-party videogame development company. In 2006, *Wired Blogs* picked the Atari VCS as one of "10 gadgets that changed the world," lauding it alongside the Sony Walkman and IBM PC. The following year, *PC World* ranked the system thirteenth on its list of "50 best tech products of all time," *Technology Review* included the Atari VCS on its list of iconic and well-designed "objects of desire," and the system took its place alongside famous toys in the Strong National Museum of Play Hall of Fame.[4]

Obviously, the Atari VCS is a cherished relic. Although no longer manufactured in its original form, it remains a living fossil. An article in *Time* in 2001 described the console's continued life after the turn of the century: "At '80s-themed parties it's common to see a 2600 wired to the TV set and guests jumping at the chance to rediscover their first videogame experience."[5] The VCS consoles have continued to come out to play, for instance, for celebrations of the thirtieth anniversary of the release of the system in late 2007. Just as a practice like letterpress printing is a contemporary, ongoing activity in addition to being the dominant method of printing from times past, the Atari VCS is admirable for its historical role in video gaming while it remains playable and programmable today.

Afterword on Platform Studies

As creative uses of the computer have blossomed in the past fifty years, studies of digital media have also been undertaken, focusing on computational artifacts, video games, and works of digital art and literature. These studies have considered creative computing in many different ways. We find it useful to distinguish five levels that characterize how the analysis of digital media has been focused—each of which, by itself, connects to contexts of culture in important ways. The levels are illustrated in figure A.1.

Reception/operation is the level that includes reception aesthetics, reader-response theory, studies based on psychoanalytic approaches, and similar methods. This level is also where media effects studies, such as desensitization to violence, and empirical studies of interaction and play are found. Although only those types of media that are interactive are explicitly operated, all sorts of media are received and understood. This means that insights from other fields can often be usefully adapted to digital media at this level. The level of reception and operation includes a wide variety of studies that are focused on the player, viewer, or reader, from the studies of Sherry Turkle to applications of Wolfgang Iser's reader-response theory and Geoffrey R. Loftus and Elizabeth F. Loftus's studies of the behavior of game players.

Interface studies include the whole discipline of human computer interaction (HCI); comparative studies of user interface done by humanistic scholars and literary critics; and approaches from visual studies, film theory, and art history. The approach that Jay David Bolter and Richard

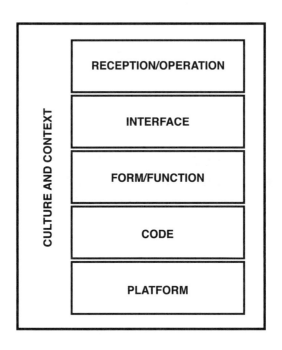

A.1 The five levels of digital media, situated in context.

Grusin have called "remediation" involves concern for interface, although reception and operation are concerns of remediation, too. This type of approach is not particularly unusual. Many studies of digital media and computer games span multiple levels, but studies often focus on one. The interface is an intriguing focus, because it is visible yet particular to interactive systems. Even if we imagine a poem or a movie as interactive, it is often not very meaningful to characterize such a work as having an interface apart from its visual or aural appearance. The interface, although an interesting layer, is what sits between the core of the program and the user; it is not the core of the program itself. A chess program may have a text interface, a speech interface, or a graphical interface, but the rules of chess and the abilities of a simulated opponent are not part of the interface.

Form/function is the level dealing with the core of the program, including the rules of the game, the nature of the simulation, and the abilities of the computer-controlled opponents. It is the main concern of cybertext studies and of much of the work characterized as game studies or ludology. Narratology, which has been used for a while to understand literature and cinema, is an approach that deals with form and function and that has been applied to digital media as well. Because these approaches deal with the same level, it is at least meaningful to imagine a narratology/ludology debate—an early conflict in game studies over whether games are better understood as essentially rule-based or narrative—while it makes much less sense to think about a psychoanalysis/ludology debate or a remediation/narratology debate.

Code is a level where explorations are still only beginning. Code studies, software studies, and code aesthetics are not yet widespread, but they are becoming known concepts. With both the Ars Electronica festival and, more recently, the Society for Literature, Science, and the Arts (SLSA) having events with code as the theme, there are more contexts for discussing the way creative work is actually programmed and the way it is understood by programmers. The discipline of software engineering is a related field that concerns itself with the code level as well as with organizational and individual capabilities for software development. Of course, looking at the source code for a particular program is very useful when considering the code level. Comments, variable names, and choices made when writing programs can be telling and can help us understand how programs were written and under what conditions. Even if the source code is not available, however, an analysis at this level of compiled code and of records of the development process can reveal many useful things.

Platform is the abstraction level beneath code, a level that has fortunately received some attention and acknowledgment, but which has not yet been systematically studied. If code studies are new media's analogue to software engineering and computer programming, platform studies are more similar to computing systems and computer architecture, connecting the fundamentals of digital media work to the cultures in which that work was done and in which coding, forms, interfaces, and eventual use are layered upon them.

As we discussed the Atari VCS, we did not shy away from mentioning some things about what games mean and how people play them, what interfaces particular games use, the particular ways that games function, and the code with which they are implemented. But though we have considered other levels, our focus in this book has been on the platform level, the one that we believe is most neglected.

We hope that our book and future studies at this level will help fill in our overall understanding of digital media and benefit the humanistic exploration of computing. We also want to emphasize again that we see all of these levels—not just the top level of reception and operation—as being situated in culture, society, economy, and history. Because of this, we sought to describe how the Atari VCS platform came about as well as how it has influenced further cultural production. A computational platform is not an alien machine, but a cultural artifact that is shaped by values and forces and which expresses views about the world, ranging from "games are typically played by two players who may be of different ages and skill levels" to "the wireless service provider, not the owner of the phone, determines what programs may be run." We hope that this awareness of the contexts of platforms has informed our approach in this book, just as it has informed the best digital media studies at other levels in the past.

We chose the Atari VCS as a starting point because it has been so influential and popular. It is also relatively simple—we were able to discuss every chip on the board in some detail without producing a technical manual. It didn't hurt that the Atari VCS remains, to us, an immensely pleasurable game system to play on, to hack on, and to program.

Platform studies is not just fun and games, though, and the approach that we are advocating doesn't apply to only the simplest computational systems. Yes, considering the platform level can certainly help illuminate other sorts of video games and game systems. Video gaming has been an extremely rich category of creative production on the computer. But consideration of the platform can also enlighten our understanding of interactive visual art, educational programs, hypertexts, works of interactive fiction, demos, creative projects in text generation, visual and kinetic poetry, and much more.

Although the Atari VCS is a platform that was originally realized in hardware, the term "platform" in general does not mean simply "hardware." There have been many influential software platforms designed to run on different sorts of boxes. In the 1970s and 1980s, BASIC became a not-quite-regularized lingua franca for the wide array of minicomputers and, later, home computers. BASIC was perhaps less principled than another beginner's language, LOGO, and was often maligned by advocates of structured programming, but it served well enough for small-scale programs and facilitated a surge in popular programming. Somehow, the "harmful" GOTO statements of the language combined with new possibilities for program distribution and the ease of access to BASIC that microcomputers provided. Studies focused on the code of particular BASIC programs are important to pursue, but studies that consider the programming language as a platform for computational expression will also be important.

BASIC is obviously not the only interesting software platform. Java, released by Sun Microsystems in 1994, has been used for business, scientific, and creative purposes and even to construct higher-level computational platforms, such as Ben Fry and Casey Reas's Processing. Although not originally a programming language, Flash, which became popular as a Macromedia product and is now an Adobe product, is a fascinating software platform that acquired computational capability as new versions were released.¹ It has been used to provide everything from professionally produced interfaces to hilarious low-brow animations and games.

Many of the early microcomputers that had BASIC built in were very interesting platforms in their own right. The Commodore 64 and Apple][were both important in the development of computer games, and, although many games were ported between the two platforms, their unique features encouraged different sorts of games to be made. The Apple][also provided a platform for advances in educational software and for the development of the first spreadsheet. The Commodore 64, on the other hand, was the first platform embraced by the demoscene, a movement that grew to be strongest in Northern Europe and that focused on programming computer-generated music videos.

There are many other significant computational platforms, from the computer-aided instruction system Programmed Logic for Automatic Teaching Operations (PLATO), which debuted in 1960, to today's mobile phones. Many are of much greater complexity than the Atari VCS. In these cases, a study the size of this book would not be able to discuss the platform technology as broadly and as deeply as we have been able to do with our chosen example. Just as it is useful to peel back layers of abstraction in a few cases, it will be useful in other cases to discuss how larger-scale systems are integrated without exploding every technical detail of every part of the system. The Atari VCS, as elegant and important as it is, cannot be used to explain how an operating system works and how that part of a system influences creative production. The console simply does not have an operating system. Other studies that don't consider chips and registers in as much detail can deal instead with this component and with other important aspects of computational platforms.

Our hopes for the future of platform studies are twofold. First, we hope that new media studies of all sorts, by curious fans and devoted scholars, will look to the platform level more often and will explore how the platform is relevant to the work, genre, or category of creative production that is being considered. It is not always obvious how to go about this, and explorations of technical details can be challenging, but already we have been provided with some good examples of platform-aware work in Alexander Galloway's *Protocol: How Control Exists after Decentralization*, Steven E. Jones's *The Meaning of Video Games*, and Matthew G. Kirschenbaum's *Mechanisms: New Media and the Forensic Imagination*. We will of course be glad if the work we have done here is useful to those undertaking studies of specific VCS games and comparative videogame studies that consider the 1977–1983 period. But we also hope that this book will serve as a more general reminder that studying what is underlying and assumed—the platform—is rewarding in all sorts of digital media research.

Beyond that, we hope that others will choose to undertake studies that center on platforms themselves. This encourages the comparison of works done on the same platform, a type of comparison we have found to be particularly fruitful. It also can lead to a more holistic view of an integrated computer system, one that wouldn't be obtained by looking at a single program or a single component. To provide a place for studies that focus on the platform level and on particular computer platforms that have influenced creative digital media work, the MIT Press is publishing the Platform Studies series, of which this book is a part.[2]

Notes

We discuss the technologies used in the Atari VCS in detail throughout the book. Our main source for information about the way the Atari VCS hardware functions and for the standard terms used to refer to parts of the system is Wright, *Stella Programmer's Guide*. A good resource for beginners is Davie, "Atari Programming for Newbies." There are several available sources of information about VCS cartridges, including the names of programmers who were not credited in the game or on the cartridge, box, or manual. Online, these include Atarimania (www.atarimania.com) and AtariAge (www.atariage.com). There is even a printed directory of VCS games (Herman, *ABC to the VCS*) that contains descriptions of more than seven hundred games, although release dates and programmer names are not provided for each game.

We also discuss many events in videogame history. Whenever we believed that there might be some question about when the event occurred or what happened, we indicated our sources in a note. We have not included citations for historical facts that are well-known and well-documented—for instance, that the original arcade game *Pac-Man* was a Namco product and was released in 1980. For general information on videogame history, there are several good books, including Burnham, *Supercade*; DeMaria and Wilson, *High Score*; Forster, *The Encyclopedia of Game Machines*; Kent, *The Ultimate History of Video Games*; and Weiss, *Classic Home Video Games, 1972–1984*. There are also many good resources online, including Herman et al., "The History of Video Games," and http://www.thegameconsole.com.

1. Stella

1. One well-known media theorist who does engage both hardware and software is Friedrich Kittler. In particular, see two essays in his collection *Media Information Systems*, "There Is No Software" and "Protected Mode."
2. Uston, *Buying and Beating the Home Video Games*, 2.

3. This sort of idea had been around in computing for a while. It was called "windowing." Ivan Sutherland developed the technique of showing one part of a drawing in his work on the 1963 system Sketchpad. This did not mean that the use of a similar concept on a television connected to an Atari VCS, or the particular mode of navigation used in *Adventure*, was straightforward or obvious.

4. Buecheler, "Haunted House."

5. In 2006 dollars, the 1982 take of arcade video games, which was $7.3 billion (Harmetz, "Hollywood Playing Harder at the Video Game"), is about $15.2 billion. By 1994, the figure had dropped to $2.3 billion, and by 2006, it had sunk to $866 million. Williams, "10 Businesses Facing Extinction in 10 Years." The total sales figure for 2006 computer and videogame software is $7.4 billion, according to the sales data from the Entertainment Software Association (http://www.theesa.com).

6. Cohen, *Zap!*, 27; Watters, "The Player."

7. Loftus and Loftus, *Mind at Play*, 10–42 passim.

8. Adams and Rollings, *Ernest Adams and Andrew Rollings on Game Design*, 46.

9. Specifically, Atari started the first pizza parlor in 1977, during the Warner years. Most of Bushnell's ideas were not being adopted by the company, but it did start a Pizza Time Theater at his suggestion. When Bushnell left, he bought the pizza business from the company. Cohen, *Zap!*, 122–123.

10. Even more ironic was Baer's development of the extremely successful handheld game *Simon*, which was based on and improved upon Atari's arcade game *Touch Me*. For a legalistic presentation of Baer's side of the story on this and other matters, see Baer, *Videogames*.

11. Atari's use of consumer components continued when *Pong* went into assembly-line production, and wasn't restricted to the display system. *Pong* unit 00–0035, as exhibited in the Boston Federal Reserve Bank in 2007, included the original container used to collect coins and the label that was on this container originally, declaring it a "Comet Standard Size Bread or Meat Loaf Pan." For a photograph of the consumer television in the first *Pong* unit, see DeMaria and Wilson, *High Score*, 20.

12. Kent, *The Ultimate History of Video Games*, 43.

13. Campbell-Kelly, *From Airline Reservations to Sonic the Hedgehog*, 273.

14. DeMaria and Wilson, *High Score!*, 26.

15. Campbell-Kelly, 274.

16. Burnham states that "approximately 200,000" were sold (*Supercade*, 82), while Baer states that the total is 350,000 (*Videogames*, 7).

17. IGN, "Atari 2600, 1977–1984."

18. Baer, 86–88.

19. Moritz, *The Little Kingdom*, 124.

20. Laing, *Digital Retro*, 15.

21. Evans, Hagiu, and Schmalensee, *Invisible Engines*, 121.

22. Goldberg, "The 2600 Story: Part I."

23. Connick, ". . . And Then There Was Apple," 24.

24. Perry and Wallich, "Design Case History."

25. The discussion that followed the blog post by Montfort, "An Atari VCS Curriculum," was particularly helpful in our thinking about important cartridges.

2 Combat

Parts of this chapter are based on Montfort, "*Combat* in Context."

1. Like many small cash businesses, including laundromats, coin-op businesses that dealt with vending machine, pinball, and arcade game distribution provided easy ways to launder money and were at times run by organized crime. This prompted increased regulation of these businesses.
2. McLuhan, "Printing and Social Change," 6.
3. NTSC is the television encoding system used in the United States, Canada, Japan, Mexico, and many other Central/South American and East Asian countries. The encoding standard used in most of Europe, much of Asia, Brazil, and about half of Africa is called PAL. A third major format, SECAM, is used in France, the other half of Africa, and the former Soviet Union. The development of PAL was necessary because North American NTSC television would not fit the 50 Hz frequency of European power grids. Because the Atari VCS does not automate its interface with the television, programmers would have to modify their programs to account for the 242 visible scan lines of a PAL television, compared with the 192 visible scan lines of an NTSC TV.
4. Wright, *Stella Programmer's Guide*, 9.
5. Berkeley, "Small Robots—Report."
6. Wardrip-Fruin, "Expressive Processing," 59–60.
7. Vavasour, "Jeff Vavasour's Video and Computer Game Page."
8. Leon, "CyberBattle 2000!"
9. O'Connor, review of *CyberBattle 2000*.
10. Langberg, review of *Combat*.
11. Bolton, review of *Combat*.

3 Adventure

1. Robinett, "Adventure as a Video Game," 692–693.
2. Robinett, 692–693.
3. Robinett, 694.
4. Robinett, 703.
5. Robinett, 694.
6. Hague, interview with Robinett in *Halcyon Days*.
7. For a thorough discussion of how fictionality and rules interact in games, see Juul, *Half-Real*.
8. Robinett, 697.
9. Hague.
10. Robinett, 704.
11. Robinett later created a diagram of *Adventure*'s space that clearly showed the disconnections between segments, but there are other ways of understanding the

game's geometric inconsistency. Caving is a matter of moving up and down in space, not just side-to-side. Because *Adventure* shows us only a two-dimensional view of the space it represents, it is possible to imagine that movement left, right, up, and down also involves movement into and out of the plane of the TV screen, as if the player were ascending and descending a sloping terrain. In such a world, the blue labyrinth would actually be under the yellow castle.

12. Kirksey, *Computer Factoids*, 114–115.
13. Hague.
14. Or, as Jim Huether said in Warshaw, *Once Upon Atari*, episode 1, "I remember when I started they just said we want you to do a game in about six months. Here's the equipment, here's the manuals, there's people around, you can ask questions. You have no set hours. We don't really want to see you until the game is almost done."
15. Hague.
16. Occasionally, writers will refer to early videogame creators as "auteurs," invoking auteur theory, which has been used to explain how individual authorship can exist in industrialized productions that have large numbers of people involved creatively. (See, for instance, Aarseth, "The Game and Its Name: What Is a Game Auteur?") It is important to note that Atari VCS programmers were not working in a context of this sort—they were literally doing all of the core creative work of game design, interface programming, core game programming, and in-game graphics and sound. Instead of making an analogy to someone like a French New Wave director with a signature style, it would be better to compare such a programmer to a filmmaker who does all the writing, cinematography, photography, sound work, editing, costuming, set dressing, and acting as well as the directing.
17. Hague.
18. Hague.
19. Montfort, *Twisty Little Passages*, 193–221.

4 Pac-Man

1. In Kohler (*Power-Up*, 22), it is noted that the story of the missing pizza slice doesn't exactly describe a real event, but that Iwatani nevertheless likes the story and tells it as if it were true.
2. Green, "Pac-Man."
3. International Arcade Museum, "Pac-Man Videogame by Midway."
4. Even today, a movable object in a 2D or 3D world is often called a sprite. And handheld systems like the Game Boy Advance and Nintendo DS, both of which evolved from the Nintendo Entertainment System, offer even more complex hardware management for sprites.
5. Rick Maurer made an important innovation in *Space Invaders* in addition to this one. He introduced a cooperative two-player mode that was very suitable for a home system and not present in any form in the arcade game.
6. Quoted in Perry and Wallich.
7. The effect is different on an LCD display, which means that an emulated *Pac-Man* game will not look the same as one played on a CRT television.
8. Townsend, "The 10 Worst Games of All Time."

9. Alexander, "Video Games Go Crunch."
10. Warshaw, *Once Upon Atari*, episode 2.
11. Control over memory banks is memory-mapped, meaning that a VCS program writes to a specific location in memory to switch from one bank to another. This can be very helpful, but is not as useful as being able to address a large memory space directly. Often, some of the contents of one bank will have to be duplicated in another because it is impractical to switch back and forth at every point where it would be necessary.
12. Available to members of the AtariAge forums at http://www.atariage.com/forums/index.php?showtopic=54937.
13. Kohler, *Power-Up*, 24.

5 *Yars' Revenge*

1. Stilphen, interview with Howard Scott Warshaw.
2. Weesner, interview with Howard Scott Warshaw.
3. Email to Montfort, 28 October 2007.
4. Larry Rosenthal was the developer of *Space Wars*. After he left Cinematronics, Tim Skelly needed to reverse-engineer the company's own product (which was not clearly documented) to determine how to create other XY graphics games of this sort. After succeeding at this, Skelly developed *Star Castle*. Skelly, "Tim Skelly's History of Cinematronics."
5. Novak, *Game Development Essentials*, 9.
6. Turkle, *The Second Self*, 84–85.
7. Poole, *Trigger Happy*, 23.
8. GameSpy, "Asteroids Gives Birth to Smack Talk."
9. That is, assuming that the color/BW console switch is set to color and a color TV is used.
10. Many emulators do now offer a mode in which pixels are blurred so that the game appears more like a CRT image, although the scan lines of the television are still not visible as they would be on original equipment. Zach Whalen has investigated the difference between the "blocky" and "fuzzy" representations of pixels in popular culture and has looked at how different display modes influence the appearance of digital images, particularly typography. Whalen, "Lost in Emulation."
11. Email to Montfort, 28 October 2007.
12. This assembly code was developed from the binary stored in ROM; Debro, "Yars_Revenge.asm."
13. Stilphen.
14. Email to Montfort, 28 October 2007.

6 *Pitfall!*

1. Fleming, "The History of Activision."
2. Fleming.
3. During a Classic Gaming Expo 2007 panel.
4. Rob Fulop, quoted in Hahn, "Favorite Atari 2600 Games." Fulop explained further in a forum posting on http://www.AtariAge.com (16 October 2007):

"After leaving Atari, Bob Smith and myself wrote a few simple editors that ran on the Atari 800. These tools enabled a graphic artist to author actual game graphics, changing both the graphics, and color, on each scan line. When they were happy with the way it all looked, the programmer ran some utility tool to add the appropriate hex codes to their program. Michael Becker was the first artist to use these tools, and he did such a great job on the set of demons that appear in Demon Attack that he became Imagic's first resident artist devoted exclusively to videogame graphics. I think it took other companies awhile to catch on to this, which is why Imagic games were known for the distinct look they have." http://www.atariage.com/forums/index.php?show topic=114992&pid=1389687&mode=threaded&start=#entry1389687.

5. Bray, *Innovation and the Communications Revolution*, 272.
6. He told this anecdote during a panel discussion at the Classic Gaming Expo 2005.
7. Email to Bogost, 23 October 2007.
8. The text continues to note that VCS games had not reached "the level of the Intellivision system," which is true, although VCS graphics capabilities exceed those of the Intellivision in some ways, as discussed at the end of the previous chapter. Of course, graphics were not the only aspect of VCS games that had significantly evolved by the beginning of the 1980s; this book continues to remark upon the advent of "multiboard plot-type games" such as *Adventure.* Uston, *Buying and Beating the Home Video Games*, 26.
9. He described this part of his interview during a panel discussion at the Classic Gaming Expo 2007.
10. All three of the games mentioned here—*Barnstorming*, *Seaquest*, and *Frostbite*—feature naturalistic settings with sunsets. VCS sunsets are discussed again at the end of chapter 6.
11. Michael Thomasson, interview with David Crane.
12. Covert, "Meet David Crane: Video Games Guru." Although *Freeway* is sometimes thought to have been inspired by *Frogger*, the two games were developed simultaneously, with the developers having no knowledge of each other's efforts.
13. This version, dubbed "Bloody Human Freeway" at AtariAge.com, is sometimes mistaken for a homebrew hack of the game.
14. Email to Bogost, 23 October 2007.
15. Email to Bogost, 23 October 2007.
16. Email to Bogost, 23 October 2007.
17. Burroughs's book *Tarzan of the Apes* was first published in a single volume in 1914, but was serialized beginning in the October 1912 issue of *All-Story*.
18. The hero of the first version of *Jungle Hunt* resembled Tarzan quite directly. The Edgar Rice Burroughs estate sued Taito over this game, called *Jungle King*, and the company renamed the game and changed the player's character to an explorer in a pith helmet. International Arcade Museum, "Jungle King Video-game by Taito."
19. Email to Bogost, 23 October 2007.
20. Email to Bogost, 23 October 2007.

21. Activision's method is clearly more aesthetically pleasing, but the less refined use of HMOVE has the side effect of making it easier for the contemporary critic or developer to see how a screen might have been drawn. Whenever that black bar appears, the HMOVE register has been strobed, usually giving a clue that the TIA has just moved some graphical object.

22. Email to Bogost, 23 October 2007. Ironically, this attention to detail didn't extend to the PAL conversion of the *Pitfall!* cartridge. The PAL video standard runs at 50 Hz rather than the 60 Hz of NTSC, which means that the *Pitfall!* timer, a critical element of the game, runs slower and "20:00" does not correspond to 20 minutes.

7 Star Wars: The Empire Strikes Back

1. That distinction goes to Atari's coin-op game *Shark Jaws*, discussed later in this chapter.
2. Email to Montfort, 24 October 2007.
3. Kent, *The Ultimate History of Video Games*, 237.
4. A delightful play on this legend is seen in the first music video from the band Wintergreen, for its 2006 song "When I Wake Up."
5. *New York Times*, "Atari Parts Are Dumped." See also Jankel and Morton, *Creative Computer Graphics*, 138.
6. Actually, only the first official game. A "Star Wars Simulation" had been programmed and was available in 1978: "Written in 14 K bytes of 8080 assembly language, the program code is offered on Tarbell and CUTS tape." *Byte*, "Star Wars Simulation."
7. Email to Montfort, 24 October 2007.
8. Email to Montfort, 5 November 2007.
9. Email to Montfort, 5 November 2007.
10. Bowen, "Musical by-products of Atari 2600 games."
11. *New York Times*, "Insider Accord in Atari Case."
12. Teiser, interoffice memo.

8 After the Crash

1. Bogost, *Persuasive Games*, 296. This was one of several examples of a VCS device that prefigured later videogame developments. Another was the GameLine modem, allowing the same sort of service that later came to be offered by the PlayStation Network, Wii Channels, and Xbox Live. Forster, "The Encyclopedia of Game Machines," 27.
2. For a detailed consideration of the challenges of emulating the VCS, see Vavasour, "Back to the Classics." In that article, the developer of the *Atari Anthology* emulator explains how he dealt with one aspect of emulation: "The Atari 2600 console had 128 different unique colors. The circuits for generating those colors are hidden inside a custom chip. Rather than guess, I created a special ROM and downloaded it into my Atari 2600. It was programmed to cycle through all the possible colors. A bar code on the top of the screen identified which color was being selected. The result was captured with a PC video card and the program

scanned the captured video, deciphering the bar code and noting the dominant color that was on the screen with it."

3. Batari Basic is a BASIC language compiler for the Atari VCS, created by Fred Quimby. It is available at http://www.bataribasic.com.

4. Null, "The 10 Gadgets that Changed the World"; Null, "The 50 Best Tech Products of All Time"; Bourzac, "Objects of Desire"; Dobbin, "Atari 2600, Raggedy Andy, Kite Enshrined."

5. Rothman, "Atari 2600."

Afterword on Platform Studies

1. Before Macromedia bought it, Flash was called FutureSplash Animator.

2. See the Web site http://www.platformstudies.com for more information on the series.

Bibliography

Texts

Aarseth, Espen. "The Game and Its Name: What Is a Game Auteur?" In *Visual Authorship: Creativity and Intentionality in Media*, edited by Torben Kragh Grodal, Bente Larsen, and Iben Thorving Laursen, 261–269. Copenhagen: Museum Tusculanum Press, 2005.

Adams, Ernest, and Andrew Rollings. *Ernest Adams and Andrew Rollings on Game Design*. New York: New Riders, 2003.

Alexander, Charles P. "Video Games Go Crunch." *Time* 122, no. 17, 17 October 1983. http://www.time.com/time/printout/0,8816,952210,00.html.

AtariAge. 1998–2008. http://www.atariage.com.

Atarimania. 2003–2008. http://www.atarimania.com/start.php.

Baer, Ralph H. *Videogames: In the Beginning*. Springfield, N.J.: Rolenta Press, 2005.

Berkeley, Edmund C. "Small Robots—Report." April 1956. http://www.blinkenlights.com/classiccmp/berkeley/report.html.

Bogost, Ian. *Persuasive Games: The Expressive Power of Video Games*. Cambridge, Mass.: MIT Press, 2007.

Bolton, Lee. "Review of *Combat*." *Lee's Peek and Poke*, 2000. http://leespeekandpoke.members.easyspace.com/combat.html.

Bourzac, Katherine. "Objects of Desire." *Technology Review*, May 2007. http://www.pcworld.com/article/id,130207-page,1-c,technology/article.html.

Bowen, Robert. "Musical By-Products of Atari 2600 Games." Form, Culture, and Video Game Criticism Conference, Princeton University, 6 March 2004.

Bray, John. *Innovation and the Communications Revolution: From the Victorian Pioneers to Broadband Internet*. London: New Riders, 2002.

Buecheler, Christopher. "Haunted House: An Atari 2600 Classic . . . and the True Progenitor of Survival Horror?" *GameSpy*, 8 December 2002. http://www.gamespy.com/articles/490/490366p1.html.

Burnham, Van. *Supercade: A Visual History of the Videogame Age 1971–1984.* Cambridge, Mass.: MIT Press, 2003.

Burroughs, Edgar Rice. *Tarzan of the Apes.* Chicago: A. C. McClurg, 1914.

Byte. "Star Wars Simulation." *Byte* 3, no. 10 (November 1978): 194.

Campbell-Kelly, Martin. *From Airline Reservations to Sonic the Hedgehog: A History of the Software Industry.* Cambridge, Mass.: MIT Press, 2003.

Cohen, Scott. *Zap!: The Rise and Fall of Atari.* Philadelphia: Xlibris Corp., [2001]. Copyright 1984.

Connick, Jack. "... And Then There Was Apple." *Call-A.P.P.L.E*, no. 24 (October 1986): 22–27.

Covert, Colin. "Meet David Crane: Video Games Guru." *Hi-Res* 1, no. 2 (January 1983): 46.

Davie, Andrew. "Atari Programming for Newbies." *AtariAge.com*, 2003. http://www.atariage.com/forums/index.php?showforum=31.

Debro, Dennis. "Yars_Revenge.asm." 21 September 2005. http://www.bjars.com/source/Yars_Revenge.asm.

Decuir, Joe. "Three Generations of Game Machine Architecture." Classic Gaming Expo, Las Vegas, Nev., 14–15 August 1999. http://www.atariarchives.org/dev/CGEXPO99.html.

DeMaria, Rusel, and Johnny Wilson. *High Score!: The Illustrated History of Electronic Games.* New York: Osborne/McGraw-Hill, 2002.

Dobbin, Ben. "Atari 2600, Raggedy Andy, Kite Enshrined." *ABC News*, 8 November 2007. http://abcnews.go.com/Technology/GadgetGuide/wireStory?id=3840526.

Dodgson, Harry, Nick Bensema, and Roger Williams. "Combat.asm." 2002. http://www.bjars.com/source/Combat.asm.

Evans, Davis S., Andrei Hagiu, and Richard Schmalensee. *Invisible Engines: How Software Platforms Drive Innovation and Transform Industries.* Cambridge, Mass.: MIT Press, 2006.

Fleming, Jeffrey. "The History of Activision." *Gamasutra*, 30 July 2007. http://www.gamasutra.com/view/feature/1537/the_history_of_activision.php.

Forster, Winnie. *The Encyclopedia of Game Machines.* London: Gameplan, 2005.

Galloway, Alexander. *Protocol: How Control Exists after Decentralization.* Cambridge, Mass.: MIT Press, 2004.

GameSpy. "Asteroids Gives Birth to Smack Talk," in "25 Smartest Moments in Gaming." *GameSpy.com*, 30 July 2007. http://archive.gamespy.com/articles/july03/25smartest/index7.shtml.

Goldberg, Marty. "The 2600 Story: Part I." *Classic Gaming/IGN*, n.d. http://classic-gaming.gamespy.com/View.php?view=Articles.Detail&id=401.

Green, Chris. "Pac-Man." *Salon.com*, 2002. http://dir.salon.com/story/ent/masterpiece/2002/06/17/pac_man/.

Guest, Judith. *Ordinary People.* New York: Viking, 1976.

Hague, James. *Halcyon Days: Interviews with Classic Computer and Video Game Programmers.* Savoy, Ill.: Dadgum Games, 1997. Free Web version, June 2002, available online at http://www.dadgum.com/halcyon/.

Hahn, Duane Alan. "Favorite Atari 2600 Games." n.d. http://www.randomterrain.com/atari-2600-memories-favorite-games.html.

Harmetz, Aljean. "Hollywood Playing Harder at the Video Game." *New York Times*, 2 August 1983, C11.

Herman, Leonard, Jer Horwitz, Steve Kent, and Skyler Miller. "The History of Video Games." *Gamespot*, n.d. http://www.gamespot.com/gamespot/features/video/hov/.

Herman, Leonard. *ABC to the VCS: A Directory of Software for the Atari 2600.* 2nd ed. Springfield, N.J.: Rolenta Press. 2005.

IGN. "Atari 2600, 1977–1984." n.d. http://classicgaming.gamespy.com/View .php?view=ConsoleMuseum.Detail&id=8&game=4.

International Arcade Museum. "Jungle King Videogame by Taito." *Killer List of Video Games*, 1995–2008. http://www.klov.com/game_detail.php?game_id=8258.

International Arcade Museum. "Pac-Man Videogame by Midway." *Killer List of Video Games*, 1995–2008. http://www.klov.com/game_detail.php?game_id=10816.

Jankel, Annabel, and Rocky Morton. *Creative Computer Graphics.* Cambridge: Cambridge University Press, 1984.

Jones, Stephen E. *The Meaning of Video Games.* London and New York: Routledge, 2008.

Juul, Jesper. *Half-Real: Video Games between Real Rules and Fictional Worlds.* Cambridge, Mass.: MIT Press, 2005.

Kent, Steven L. *The Ultimate History of Video Games.* New York: Prima, 2001.

Kittler, Friedrich. Literature, Media, Information Systems. Ed. John Johnston. New York: Routledge, 1997.

Kirksey, Kirk. *Computer Factoids: Tales from the High-Tech Underbelly.* Lincoln, Neb.: iUniverse, 2005.

Kirschenbaum, Matthew. *Mechanisms: New Media and the Forensic Imagination.* Cambridge, Mass.: MIT Press, 2008.

Kohler, Chris. *Power-Up: How Japanese Video Games Gave the World an Extra Life.* Indianapolis: Brady Games, 2004.

Laing, Gordon. *Digital Retro.* London: Ilex, 2004.

Langberg, Ben. Review of *Combat Le Geek*, 2003. http://abscape.org/legeek/r_combat .htm.

Leon, Harmon. "CyberBattle 2000!" *DailyRadar.com*, 2000. Original site offline, see http://web.archive.org/web/*/http://www.dailyradar.com/features/showbiz_ feature_page_84_1.html.

Loftus, Geoffrey R., and Elizabeth F. Loftus. *Mind at Play: The Psychology of Video Games.* New York: Basic Books, 1983.

McLuhan, Marshall. "Printing and Social Change." Vol. 1 of *Marshall McLuhan Unbound.* Corte Madera, Calif.: Gingko Press, 2005.

Montfort, Nick. *Twisty Little Passages: An Approach to Interactive Fiction.* Cambridge, Mass.: MIT Press, 2003.

Montfort, Nick. "An Atari VCS Curriculum." *Grand Text Auto*, 6 July 2004. http:// grandtextauto.org/2004/06/06/an-atari-vcs-curriculum/.

Montfort, Nick. "*Combat* in Context." *Game Studies* 6, no. 1 (2006). http://gamestudies .org/0601/articles/montfort.

Moritz, Michael. *The Little Kingdom: The Private Story of Apple Computer.* New York: William Morrow, 1984.

New York Times. "Atari Parts Are Dumped." 28 September 1983, D4.

New York Times. "Insider Accord In Atari Case." 6 June 1984.

Novak, Jeannie. *Game Development Essentials: An Introduction.* Clifton Park, N.Y.: Thomson Delmar, 2004.

Null, Christopher. "The 10 Gadgets that Changed the World." *Wired Blogs*, 12 December 2006. http://www.wired.com/gadgets/miscellaneous/multimedia/2006/12/wiredphotos6.

Null, Christopher. "The 50 Best Tech Products of All Time." *PC World*, 2 April 2007. http://www.pcworld.com/article/id,130207-page,1-c,technology/article.html.

O'Connor, Frank. Review of *CyberBattle 2000*. [Parody review of *Combat*.] *DailyRadar .com*, 2000. Original site offline, see http://web.archive.org/web/*/http://www .dailyradar.com/reviews/game_review_693.html.

Perry, Tekla, and Paul Wallich. "Design Case History: The Atari Video Computer System." *IEEE Spectrum* 20, no. 3 (1983): 45–51.

Poole, Stephen. *Trigger Happy: Videogames and the Entertainment Revolution*. New York: Arcade Publishing, 2000.

Puzo, Mario. *The Godfather*. New York: Putnam, 1969.

Robinett, Warren. "Adventure as a Video Game: Adventure for the Atari 2600." In *The Game Design Reader*, ed. Katie Salen and Eric Zimmerman. Cambridge, Mass.: MIT Press, 2006.

Rothman, Wilson. "Atari 2600." *Time*, 11 March 2001. http://www.time.com/time/magazine/article/0,9171,102027,00.html.

Skelly, Tim. "Tim Skelly's History of Cinematronics." 1 June 1999. http://www .dadgum.com/giantlist/archive/cinematronics.html.

Stilphen, Scott. Interview with Howard Scott Warshaw. 23 April 2005. http://www .digitpress.com/archives/interview_warshaw.htm.

thegameconsole.com. "A Brief History of the Home Video Game Console." http:// www.thegameconsole.com.

Teiser, Don. Interoffice memo to John De Santis. *AtariMuseum.com*, 14 June 1983. http://www.atarimuseum.com/articles/atari-nintendo-deal.htm.

Thomasson, Michael. Interview with David Crane. *Good Deal Games*, 2003. http:// www.gooddealgames.com/interviews/int_David_Crane.html.

Townsend, Emru. "The 10 Worst Games of All Time." *PC World*, 23 October 2006. http://www.pcworld.com/printable/article/id,127579/printable.html.

Turkle, Sherry. *The Second Self: Computers and the Human Spirit*. New York: Simon & Schuster, 1984.

Uston, Ken. *Ken Uston's Guide to Buying and Beating the Home Video Games*. New York: Signet, 1982.

Vavasour, Jeff. "Back to the Classics: Perfecting the Emulation for Digital Eclipse's Atari Anthology." *Gamasutra*, 13 January 2004. http://www.gamasutra.com/features/20050113/vavasour_pfv.htm.

Vavasour, Jeff. "Jeff Vavasour's Video and Computer Game Page." 2008. http://www .vavasour.ca/jeff/games.html.

Wardrip-Fruin, Noah. "Expressive Processing: On Process-Intensive Literature and Digital Media." Ph.D. diss, Brown University, 2006.

Watters, Ethan. "The Player." *Wired* 13, no. 10 (October 2005). http://www.wired .com/wired/archive/13.10/bushnell_pr.html.

Weesner, Jason. Interview with Howard Scott Warshaw. 29 May 2007. http://www .gamecareerguide.com/features/378/on_game_design_the_.php?page=2.

Weiss, Brett. *Classic Home Video Games, 1972–1984*. New York: McFarland, 2007.

Whalen, Zach. "Lost in Emulation: World of Difference in Videogame Typography." 3rd Annual UF Game Studies Conference, Gainesville, Fla., 1 March 2007.

Williams, Geoff. "10 Businesses Facing Extinction in 10 Years." *Entrepreneur*, 19 September 2007. http://www.entrepreneur.com/extinction/index.html.

Wright, Steve. *Stella Programmer's Guide*. 3 December 1979. Reconstructed by Charles Sinnett, 11 June 1993. http://www.atarihq.com/danb/files/stella.pdf.

Video Games

This section of the bibliography is organized by author. Whoever was originally credited as author of a video game when the game was originally released is considered to be the author for the purposes of this list. Since policies for attributing authorship vary, "Atari" is the author of all games published by that company, while individuals were considered the authors of Activision games. In all cases, including when games have a corporate author, we have indicated, to the best of our knowledge, the people who programmed, designed, and did other work on these games.

Amstar Electronics. *Phoenix*. Arcade. Distributed by Centauri. 1980.

Atari. *Pong*. Arcade. Designed by Nolan Bushnell. Engineered by Al Alcorn. 1972.

Atari. *Gran Trak 10*. Arcade. 1974.

Atari. *Touch Me*. Arcade. 1974.

Atari. *Anti-Aircraft*. Arcade. 1975.

Atari. *Home Pong*. Engineered by Al Alcorn, Bob Brown, and Harold Lee. 1975.

Atari. *Breakout*. Arcade. Designed by Nolan Bushnell and Steve Bristow. Engineered by Gary Waters and Steve Wozniak. 1976.

Atari. *Night Driver*. Arcade. Programmed by Dave Shepperd. Engineered by Ron Milner, Steve Mayer, and Terry Fowler. 1976.

Atari. *Air-Sea Battle*. Atari VCS. Programmed by Larry Kaplan. 1977.

Atari. *Basic Math*. Atari VCS. Programmed by Gary Palmer. 1977.

Atari. *Blackjack*. Atari VCS. Programmed by Bob Whitehead. 1977.

Atari. *Combat*. Atari VCS. Programmed by Joe Decuir and Larry Wagner. 1977.

Atari. *Indy 500*. Atari VCS. Programmed by Ed Riddle. 1977.

Atari. *Star Ship*. Atari VCS. Programmed by Bob Whitehead. 1977.

Atari. *Street Racer*. Atari VCS. Programmed by Larry Kaplan. 1977.

Atari. *Surround*. Atari VCS. Programmed by Alan Miller. 1977.

Atari. *Video Olympics*. Atari VCS. Programmed by Joe Decuir. 1977.

Atari. *Breakout*. Atari VCS. Programmed by Brad Stewart. 1978.

Atari. *Slot Racers*. Atari VCS. Programmed by Warren Robinett. 1978.

Atari. *Asteroids*. Arcade. Developed by Ed Logg and Lyle Rains. 1979.

Atari. *Basic Programming*. Atari VCS. Programmed by Warren Robinett. 1979.

Atari. *Basketball*. Atari VCS. Programmed by Alan Miller. 1979.

Atari. *Lunar Lander*. Arcade. 1979.

Atari. *Superman*. Atari VCS. Programmed by John Dunn. 1979.

Atari. *Video Chess*. Atari VCS. Programmed by Larry Kaplan and Bob Whitehead. 1979.

Atari. *Adventure*. Atari VCS. Programmed by Warren Robinett. 1980.

Atari. *Battlezone*. Arcade. Programmed by Ed Rotberg. 1980.

Atari. *Missile Command*. Arcade. 1980.

Atari. *Space Invaders*. Atari VCS. Programmed by Rick Maurer. 1980.

Atari. *Tempest*. Arcade. Programmed by David Theurer. 1980.

Atari. *Asteroids*. Atari VCS. Programmed by Brad Stewart. 1981.

Atari. *Defender*. Atari VCS. Programmed by Bob Polaro. 1981.

Atari. *Yars' Revenge*. Atari VCS. Programmed by Howard Scott Warshaw. 1981.

Atari. *E.T.: The Extra-Terrestrial*. Atari VCS. Programmed by Howard Scott Warshaw. 1982.

Atari. *Haunted House*. Atari VCS. Programmed by James Andreasen. 1982.

Atari. *Pac-Man*. Atari VCS. Programmed by Tod Frye. 1982.

Atari. *Raiders of the Lost Ark*. Atari VCS. Programmed by Howard Scott Warshaw. 1982.

Atari. *Realsports Boxing*. Atari VCS. 1987.

Atari. *Atari Anthology*. PlayStation 2 and Xbox. 2004.

Bally Midway. *Tron*. Arcade. Engineered by Atish Ghos. Programmed by Bill Adams. Art by George Gomez. 1982.

Bally Midway. *Jr. Pac-Man*. Arcade. 1983.

Blizzard Entertainment. *Warcraft: Orcs & Humans*. Mac System 7 and PC. 1994.

Blizzard Entertainment. *Warcraft III: Reign of Chaos*. Mac OS 9, Mac OS X, and Windows. Designed by Rob Pardo. 2002.

Blizzard Entertainment. *World of Warcraft*. Mac OS X and Windows. 2004–present.

Burness, Jack. *Lunar Lander*. PDP-11 program. Commissioned by DEC. 1973.

Bushnell, Nolan. *Computer Space*. Arcade. Distributed by Nutting Associates. 1971.

Cartwright, Steve. *Barnstorming*. Atari VCS. Activision, 1981.

Cartwright, Steve. *Seaquest*. Atari VCS. Activision, 1982.

Cartwright, Steve. *Frostbite*. Atari VCS. Activision, 1983.

Cinematronics. *Star Castle*. Arcade. 1977.

Cinematronics. *Space Wars*. Arcade. 1977.

Coleco. *Telstar Combat!* Dedicated. 1977.

Core Design Ltd. *Tomb Raider*. Macintosh, PlayStation, PC, and Sega Saturn. Eidos, 1996.

Crane, David. *Freeway*. Atari VCS. Activision, 1981.

Crane, David. *Grand Prix*. Atari VCS. Activision, 1982.

Crane, David. *Pitfall!* Atari VCS. Activision, 1982.

Crowther, Will, and Don Woods. *Adventure*. PDP-10 Fortran. 1976.

Data Age. *Journey Escape*. Atari VCS. 1982.

Davie, Andrew. *Qb*. Atari VCS. 2003.

DSD/Camelot. *Tooth Protectors*. For Johnson & Johnson, 1983.

Electronic Arts. *The Godfather: The Game*. PlayStation 2, PlayStation 3, PSP, Xbox, Xbox 360, Wii, Windows. 2006.

Exus. *Video Jogger*. Atari VCS. 1987.

Exus. *Video Reflex*. Atari VCS. 1987.

Garriott, Richard (as Lord British). *Ultima I: The First Age of Darkness*. Apple][. Origin Systems, 1980.

Garriott, Richard (as Lord British). *Ultima IV: Quest of the Avatar*. Apple][and many other home computers and consoles. Origin Systems, 1985.

General Computing Corporation. *Ms. Pac-Man*. Distributed by Bally Midway, 1982.

Google. *Google Earth*. Web and downloadable application with video game Easter egg. 2004–present.

Gremlin. *Blockade*. Arcade. 1976.

Hasboro Interactive. *Atari Arcade Hits: Volume 1*. Programmed and produced by Jeff Vavasour. Windows. 1999.

Higinbotham, William. *Tennis for Two*. Developed at the Brookhaven National Labora-
    tory. 1958.
id Software. *Quake*. PC. 1996.
Imagic. *Demon Attack*. Atari VCS. Programmed by Rob Fulop. Art by Michael Becker.
    1982.
Exidy. *Death Race*. Arcade. Engineered by Howell Ivey. 1976.
Jentzsch, Thomas. *Thrust*. Atari VCS. XYPE. 2003.
Jentzsch, Thomas. *Jammed*. Atari VCS. XYPE. 2004.
Kaplan, Larry, and David Crane. *Kaboom!* Atari VCS. Activision. 1981.
Kee Games. *Tank*. Arcade. Engineered by Steve Bristow and Lyle Rains. 1974.
Kee Games. *Sprint 2*. Arcade. 1976.
Kee Games. *Sprint 1*. Arcade. 1978.
Kitchen, Garry. *Pressure Cooker*. Atari VCS. Activision. 1983.
Kitchen, Steve. *Space Shuttle: A Journey into Space*. Atari VCS. Activision.
    1983.
Konami. *Track & Field*. Atari VCS. Programmed by Jaques Hugon and Seth
    Lipkin. 1984.
Konami. *Dance Dance Revolution*. Arcade. 1998.
Konami. *Dance Dance Revolution 2nd Mix*. Dreamcast and PlayStation. 1999.
Lebling, Dave, Marc Blanc, Timothy Anderson, and Bruce Daniels. *Zork*. PDP-10.
    1979.
Lebling, Dave, and Marc Blanc. *Zork*. Z-Machine. Infocom. 1980.
Logg, Ed, and Dona Bailey. *Centipede*. Atari. 1980.
M Network. *Kool-Aid Man*. Atari VCS and Intellivision. Mattel Electronics.
    1983.
Mattel. *Simon*. Handheld game. Engineered by Ralph Baer. 1978.
Mayer, Steve, Dave Shepperd, and Dennis Koble. *Starship 1*. Atari. 1977.
Mayfield, Mike. *Star Trek*. SDS Sigma 7 and HP minicomputers. 1971.
Maxis. *SimCity*. PC and Commodore 64. Programmed by Will Wright. Brøderbund.
    1989.
Meier, Sid. *Civilization*. PC, Macintosh, and other home computers. MicroProse.
    1991.
Microsoft. *Excel*. Macintosh and Windows application with video game Easter Egg.
    1985.
Midway. *Sea Wolf*. Arcade. 1976.
Midway. *Defender*. Arcade. Developed by Eugene Jarvis. 1980.
Midway. *Gorf*. Arcade. 1981.
Mullich, David. *The Prisoner*. Apple][. EduWare. 1980.
Mystique. *Bachelor Party*. Mystique. 1982.
Mystique. *Beat 'Em and Eat 'Em*. Atari VCS. 1982.
Mystique. *Custer's Revenge*. Atari VCS. 1982.
Namco. *Galaxian*. Arcade. Distributed by Midway. 1979.
Namco. *Pac-Man*. Arcade. 1980.
Namco. *Galaga*. Arcade. Distributed by Midway. 1981.
Namco. *Rally X*. Arcade. 1981.
Neversoft. *Tony Hawk Pro Skater*. Activision, 1999.
Nintendo. *Super Mario Bros*. Nintendo Entertainment System. Designed by Shigeru
    Miyamoto. 1985.

Nintendo. *The Legend of Zelda*. Nintendo Entertainment System. Designed by Shigeru Miyamoto. 1986.

Nintendo. *Super Mario 64*. Nintendo 64. 1996.

Nintendo. *Wii Sports*. Wii. 2006.

Parker Brothers. *Amidar*. Atari VCS. Programmed by Ed Temple. 1982.

Parker Brothers. *Frogger*. Atari VCS. Programmed by Ed English. 1982.

Parker Brothers. *Spider-Man*. Atari VCS. Programmed by Laura Nikolich. 1982.

Parker Brothers. *Star Wars: The Empire Strikes Back*. Atari VCS. Programmed by Rex Bradford and Sam Kjellman. 1982.

Parker Brothers. *Sky Skipper*. Atari VCS. 1983.

Parker Brothers. *Star Wars: Jedi Arena*. Atari VCS. Programmed by Rex Bradford. 1983.

Parker Brothers. *Strawberry Shortcake Musical Matchups*. Atari VCS. Programmed by Dawn Stockbridge. 1983.

Parker Brothers. *Super Cobra*. Atari VCS. Programmed by Mike Brodie. 1982.

Rockstar Games. *Grand Theft Auto: San Andreas*. PlayStation 2, Windows, and Xbox. Take Two, 2004.

Russell, Steve, Martin Graetz, and Wayne Wiitanen. *Spacewar*. PDP-1. Developed at MIT. 1962.

Shaw, Carol. *River Raid*. Atari VCS. Activision, 1982.

Slocum, Paul. *Combat Rock*. Atari VCS. 2002.

Slocum, Paul. *Synthcart*. Atari VCS. 2002.

Spectravision. *Chase the Chuck Wagon*. Atari VCS. For Ralston-Purina, 1983.

Taito. *Space Invaders*. Distributed by Midway, 1978.

Taito. *Jungle Hunt*. Distributed by Midway, 1982.

Thornton, Adam (as One of the Bruces). *Lord of the Rings: The Fellowship of the Ring*. Atari VCS. 2002.

Toy, Michael, Ken Arnold, and Glenn Wichman. *Rogue*. Unix, PC, and Macintosh. 1980.

Troutman, Greg. *Dark Mage*. Atari VCS. 1998.

Twentieth Century Fox. *Porky's*. Atari VCS. 1982.

Valve. *Half-Life*. PC and PlayStation 2. Sierra Entertainment. 1998.

Valve. *Half-Life 2*. Windows, Xbox, Xbox 360, and PlayStation 3. Valve Corporation. 2004.

Vatical Entertainment. *Yars' Revenge*. Game Boy Color. Telegames. 1999.

Velocity Development. *Spectre*. Peninsula Gameworks. 1991.

Whitehead, Bob. *Boxing*. Atari VCS. Activision. 1980.

Whitehead, Bob. *Skiing*. Atari VCS. Activision. 1980.

Wizard Video Games. *Halloween*. Atari VCS. 1983.

Wizard Video Games. *The Texas Chainsaw Massacre*. Atari VCS. Programmed by Ed Salvo. 1983.

Yob, Gregory. *Hunt the Wumpus*. BASIC. 1972.

Motion Pictures

Bartel, Paul. *Death Race 2000*. New World. 1975.

Clark, Bob. *Porky's*. Twentieth Century Fox. 1982.

Coppola, Francis Ford. *The Godfather*. Paramount Pictures. 1972.

Lisberger, Steven. *Tron*. Disney. 1982.

Lucas, George. *Star Wars*. Fox Pictures. 1977.

Lucas, George. *Star Wars: The Empire Strikes Back*. Fox Pictures. 1980.

Redford, Robert. *Ordinary People*. Paramount Pictures. 1980.

Spielberg, Steven. *Jaws*. Universal Pictures. 1975.

Warshaw, Howard Scott. *Once Upon Atari*. 2003.

Index